Grades 3 & 4

An Unofficial Activity Book

The Super Fun Colossal Workbook for

MINECRAFTERS

SKY PONY PRESS

Sky Pony Press
New York

Copyright © 2021 by Hollan Publishing, Inc.
Minecraft® is a registered trademark of Notch Development AB.

The Minecraft game is copyright © Mojang AB.

Sky Pony Press books may be purchased in bulk at special discounts for sales promotion, corporate gifts, fund-raising, or educational purposes. Special editions can also be created to specifications. For details, contact the Special Sales Department, Sky Pony Press, 307 West 36th Street, 11th Floor, New York, NY 10018 or info@skyhorsepublishing.com.

Sky Pony® is a registered trademark of Skyhorse Publishing, Inc.®, a Delaware corporation.

Visit our website at www.skyponypress.com.

10 9 8 7 6 5 4 3

Library of Congress Cataloging-in-Publication Data is available on file.

Print ISBN: 978-1-5107-6304-3

Cover design by Kai Texel
Interior design by Noora Cox
Cover and interior illustrations by Amanda Brack

Printed in China

A NOTE TO PARENTS

Welcome to a super world of colossal fun and learning with a Minecrafting twist. When you want to reinforce classroom skills, break up screen time, or enhance kids' problem-solving skills at home, it's crucial to have high-interest, kid-friendly learning materials.

The Super Fun Colossal Workbook for Minecrafters transforms educational lessons into exciting adventures complete with diamond swords, zombies, skeletons, and creepers. With colorful illustrations and familiar characters to guide them through, your kids will feel like winners from start to finish. The best part: The educational content in this workbook is aligned with National Common Core Standards for 3rd and 4th grade. So everything in this book matches up with what your children are learning and will be learning—to build confidence and keep them ahead of the curve.

Whether it's the joy of seeing their favorite game come to life on each page or the thrill of solving challenging problems just like Steve and Alex, there is something in *The Super Fun Colossal Workbook for Minecrafters* to engage every kind of learner. Happy adventuring!

CONTENTS

SOCIAL SKILLS FOR MINECRAFTERS................................**4**

STEM QUEST CHALLENGES*.....................................**43**

MATH FOR MINECRAFTERS...**98**

READING FOR MINECRAFTERS................................**165**

WRITING FOR MINECRAFTERS.................................**221**

PUZZLES AND GAMES FOR MINECRAFTERS.............**288**

ANSWER KEY...**343**

CARDS FOR BOUNCE BACK GAME.........................**355**

* While all of these projects are kid-friendly and encourage little ones to get involved, some of the experiments require or strongly benefit from parental supervision.

SOCIAL SKILLS
FOR MINECRAFTERS

CREEPER AND YOU

Read about creeper. Then write about yourself.

	CREEPER	YOU
PHYSICAL DESCRIPTION	Creeper is made up of green and gray blocks. It has two black eyes and a black mouth on its large block head. It has a long body with no arms. It has two blocks for feet.	
LIKES	gunpowder, music, mob heads	
DISLIKES	bows, ocelots, cats	
TALENTS/ STRENGTHS	chasing players, hissing, exploding	

Have you seen a creeper when playing Minecraft? If so, write about what happened. If not, write about what you imagine would happen.

_____

_____

_____

_____

ME IN PIXELS

Use the grid paper to create an image of yourself,
a selfie, in pixels.

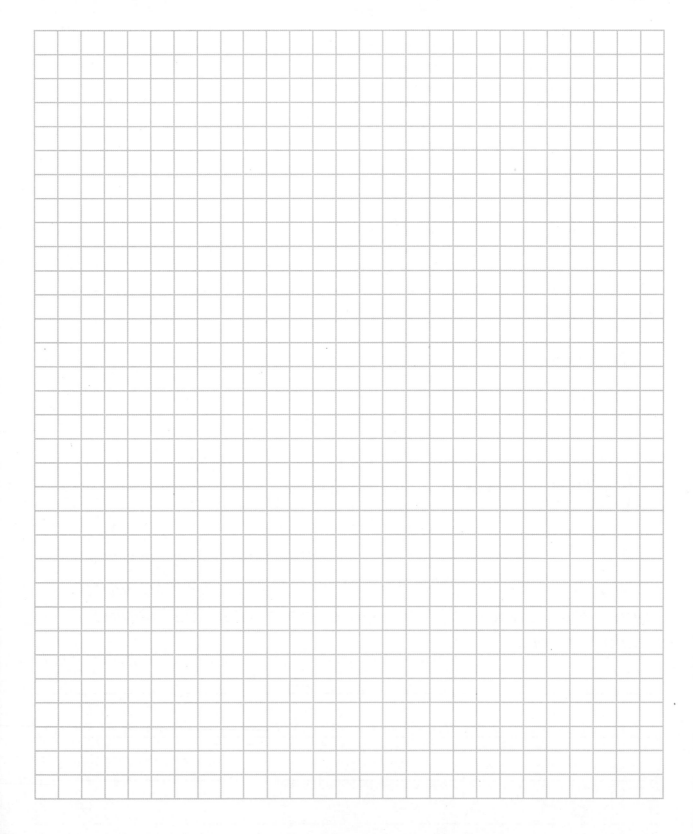

WHAT DO YOU VALUE?

In the Minecraft world, valuable items help you survive. What you value are the people and things that you think are important. One way to understand what you value is by looking at what rules your family has and how you spend your time. What you value says a lot about you.

Valuable in Minecraft

What rules does your family have?	How does your family spend their time?

What do you value?

POWERFUL WORD PORTAL

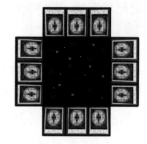

Adjectives are words that describe people and things. The words you use to describe yourself have power, so choose them carefully!

Circle the adjectives in this word puzzle, and then star the ones that best describe you.

WORD LIST:

ATHLETIC

BRAVE

CREATIVE

FRIENDLY

FUNNY

HONEST

KIND

LOYAL

SMART

STRONG

Q	V	F	U	N	N	Y	Z	W	B
H	M	U	M	A	S	G	K	R	R
C	S	Y	F	T	T	T	I	F	A
Z	R	O	O	H	R	J	N	R	V
H	S	E	Z	L	O	U	D	I	E
O	M	F	A	E	N	N	A	E	T
N	A	Q	K	T	G	U	G	N	I
E	R	S	N	I	I	P	J	D	K
S	T	M	K	C	K	V	X	L	E
T	L	O	Y	A	L	K	E	Y	D

POSITIVE POETRY

If you say kind things about yourself, you'll start *feeling* better about yourself, too.

Write a poem made up of positive words that start with the letters of your first name. Here's an example:

G: Generous

O: Observant

L: Loyal

E: Energetic

M: Mighty

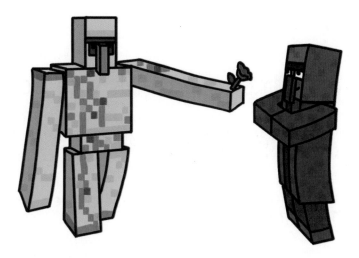

Your turn! Write the letters of your first name in the squares, and come up with positive words that describe you starting with those letters.

☐ _____   ☐ _____

☐ _____   ☐ _____

☐ _____   ☐ _____

☐ _____   ☐ _____

☐ _____   ☐ _____

WATCH FOR CREEPERS

Sometimes unkind thoughts creep into our minds when we're not paying attention. Are you calling yourself names or saying you can't do something? Talk back to that voice in your head!

For every negative thought below, turn it into something positive.

No one wants to be friends with me.

I'm a good friend because _____.

People don't like me.

People like that I _____.

I'll never be good at that.

I'll get better at _____ **if I** _____.

I'm such a loser!

I'm such a good _____.

I can't do it.

I can _____ **if I keep trying.**

WHO'S GOT YOUR BACK?

We all need people to rely on. Think about friends, family members, teachers, coaches, and other people who support you.

How do they make you feel good about yourself?
How do you do the same for them?

These are people who help me feel good about myself:

_____ _____ _____

They make me feel appreciated when they _____

_____.

I make them feel good when I _____

_____.

Here's something kind someone did for me: _____

_____.

Here's something I can do to thank them:_____

_____.

WHEN STRESS STRIKES

It's hard to feel confident when you're scared or stressed. Are you stressed out? Do you recognize the signs?

Check off anything in the list that sounds like you:

- [ ] My hands feel sweaty a lot.
- [ ] I have trouble sleeping.
- [ ] I get stomachaches every day.
- [ ] I can't catch my breath.
- [ ] I'm always tired.
- [ ] I'm not hungry at mealtime.
- [ ] I snack more than usual.
- [ ] My throat feels tight.
- [ ] My chest feels tight.
- [ ] I get angry easily.
- [ ] I cry often.
- [ ] I can't concentrate at school.

ALL of these can be signs of stress. If you checked **5 or more** boxes, let an adult know that you're feeling stressed. Then keep reading for ways to *stop* stress in its tracks.

HEALTH METER QUIZ

Feeling happy, confident, and stress-free starts with a healthy body. How well are you taking care of your body?

Check the statements that are true about you:

☐ I eat breakfast most days.

☐ I sleep 9 or 10 hours most nights.

☐ I'm active (at recess, in sports, or playing at home) for at least an hour a day.

☐ At dinnertime, I drink water or milk instead of juice or soda.

☐ I take a bath or shower at least two or three times a week.

*For every check you made above, color in **2** hearts below.*

Now turn the page to see what your health meter is telling you...

How did you do?

8 to 10 hearts: You're taking great care of your body! That's the first step to feeling *happy*, too.

4 to 6 hearts: You have some healthy habits, but there's more you could do for a healthy body—and mind. Choose one thing from the list that you can try today.

0 to 2 hearts: You're running on empty! Share this checklist with a parent or adult who can help you start taking better care of your body.

DON'T BE A ZOMBIE

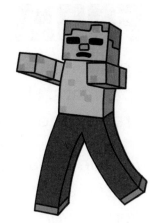

If you don't get enough sleep at night, you'll struggle to make it through your day.

Try these tips for getting enough zzz's:

❋ Steer clear of caffeine in the afternoon and evening. No soda or hot chocolate!

❋ Follow the same routine every night, such as taking a shower, brushing your teeth, and reading a book or listening to music.

What's your routine? Write it here:

_____

_____

_____

_____

_____

❋ Once you're in bed, take a few deep breaths. Count to 3 as you inhale, hold the breath for 3 seconds, and count to 3 as you exhale. Imagine that you're breathing in cool confidence and breathing out stress and worry.

FROM A TO ZZZ

Sometimes at night, our minds spin like mob spawners. How do you make it stop? Give your brain something else to do.

Try the Minecraft alphabet game. For each letter, think of a mob, critter, enchantment, or item that starts with that letter. (You've been given a head start!)

A: <u>Axe</u>

B: _____

C: _____

D: _____

E: _____

F: <u>Fireworks</u>

G: _____

H: _____

I: _____

J: _____

K: <u>Knockback enchantment</u>

L: Llama _____

M: _____

N: _____

O: _____

P: _____

Q: Quartz _____

R: _____

S: _____

T: _____

U: Unbreaking enchantment _____

V: _____

W: _____

X: _____

Y: _____

Z: X marks the spot! _____

Want to play an easier version? The next time you're lying in bed awake at night, try to think of a Minecraft mob, critter, or item for every color in the rainbow. Red parrots, orange lava...and so on!

MESS = STRESS, CLEAN = CONFIDENCE

To feel less stressed and more confident, clean your room! Rearrange it, or decorate it the way you'd decorate a house in Minecraft.

Practice by coloring in the room below, adding each item in this list:

❋ A painting on the wall

❋ A colorful bedspread

❋ A patterned rug

❋ Window curtains

❋ A soft lamp or torch

❋ Flowers

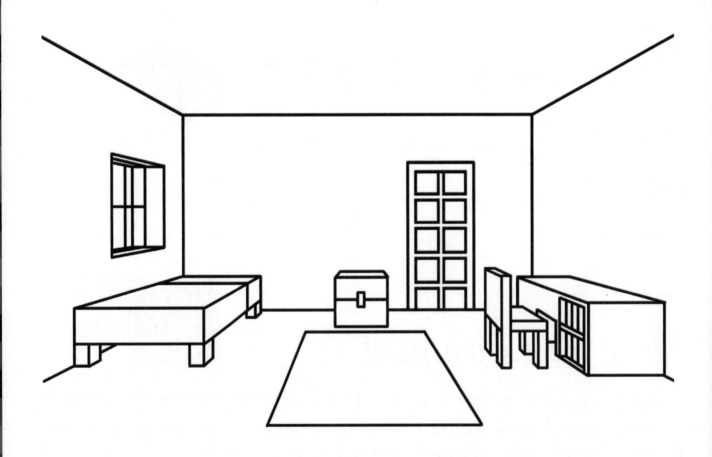

BE-FRIEND YOURSELF

If your confidence starts to slip, give yourself a pep talk—just like you would with a friend. If you practice speaking kindly to yourself, you'll have the words to use whenever you need a boost.

Fill in the blanks below.

[Your name here] _____,

I really like how you _____,

_____, and _____.

You're already good at _____. And you've

been practicing _____, so I know

you're going to get better and better.

[Your name here] _____, you rock!

TACKLE TINY GOALS

Need more fun ways to boost your confidence?

Check off the things you'd like to try:

☐ Save money for something special. Decorate
a small box to look like a treasure chest and add a slot on
top for gold ingots—er, dollars and coins!

☐ Draw a comic strip featuring you as a superhero or a
master Minecrafter.

☐ Build a house out of playing cards instead of Minecraft blocks.

☐ Map out an obstacle course at a playground that you can
do without touching the ground. (Imagine that you're in
the Nether, and the ground is hot lava!) Time yourself and
try to get faster each time you complete the course.

☐ Taste a food you've never tried before. (Mushroom stew,
anyone?) Take at least three bites.

☐ Make up a tongue twister about spiders spawning in sand.
Add as many "s" words as you can.

AIM HIGH!

Bigger goals take time and effort, but you feel really good when you meet them—and ready to tackle the next one on your list. So set your sights high.

What do you want to do? Choose one of these goals, or add your own.

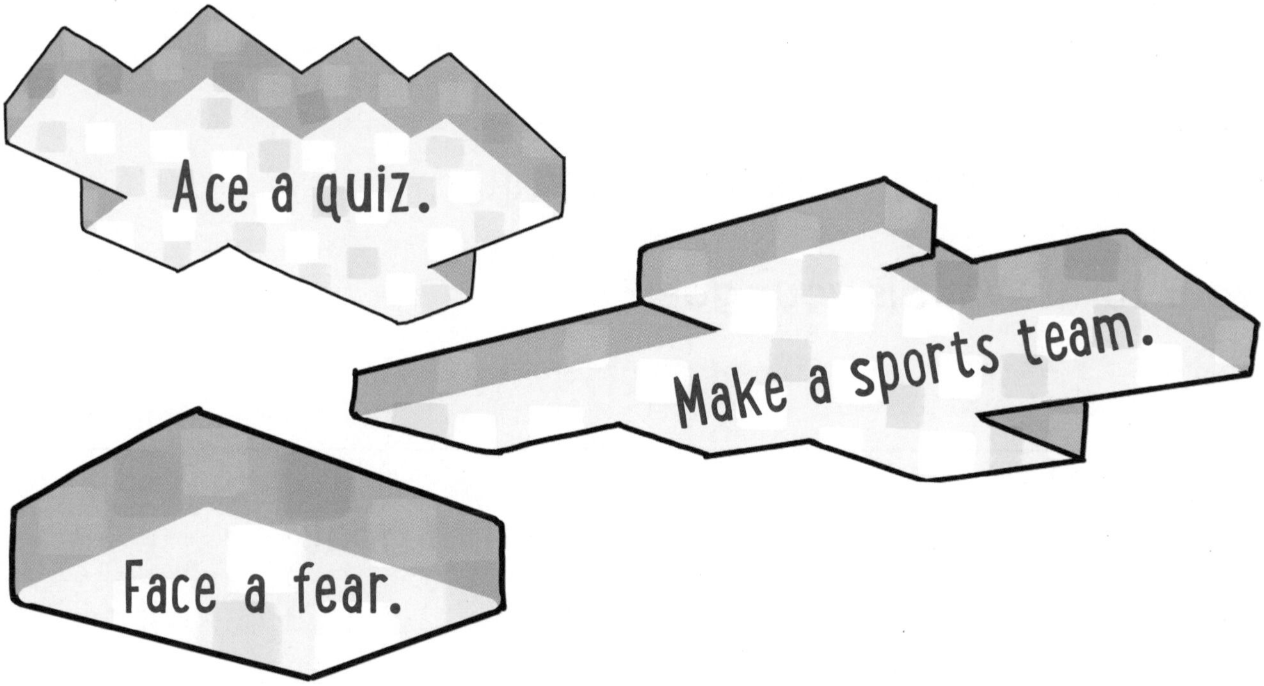

Ace a quiz.

Make a sports team.

Face a fear.

Your goal: _____

Your goal: _____

Your goal: _____

STEPS TO SUCCESS

Choose a goal from the previous page, and break it down into small steps. If your goal is to ace a spelling quiz, your steps might look like this:

❋ Set up a study schedule.

❋ Make flash cards.

❋ Find a buddy to practice with.

❋ Practice for 30 minutes every night after school.

❋ Get a good night's sleep before the quiz.

Your turn! What is your goal?

_____

List 5 steps you can take to reach that goal:

1. _____

2. _____

3. _____

4. _____

5. _____

PICK YOUR TEAM

Sometimes reaching goals takes teamwork. Don't be afraid to ask for help!

Think of at least one person for each of the "teammates" below:

❋ The cheerleader who picks me up when I'm

feeling down: _____

❋ The coach who gives me great advice: _____

❋ The teammate who will work hard with me:

_____

❋ The friend who makes everything more fun:

_____

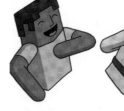

❋ The people who will celebrate with me when I reach my goal:

_____, _____,

and _____

SPEAK UP (BEFORE YOU BLOW UP!)

If a friend isn't treating you well, do you stay silent? Or bottle up your anger until you blow sky high? There's a better way to let your friend know how you feel.

• Start with the words "I feel..." instead of "You always (do this or that)..." That way, your friend won't feel like you're pointing the finger and might be more likely to listen.

• Describe WHEN you feel that way, such as "when you play with other kids and don't invite me." Be specific! Your friend can't read your mind.

• Give your friend a chance to make things better. What do you want your friend to do differently? Try "I'd feel better if you would ask me to join you."

Think of something that's been bothering you. How can you let a friend know what you need? Fill in the blanks below:

I feel _____ when you _____

_____. I would

feel better if you _____ instead.

FRIEND OR FOE?

Does a friend keep saying or doing something hurtful? It's time to decide if this person is *really* a friend.

Check off everything that sounds like your friend below.

My friend...

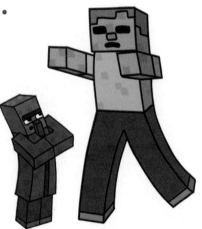

- ☐ Has shared my secrets with other people.

- ☐ Leaves me out of things often.

- ☐ Has called me names.

- ☐ Gets mad if I play with anybody else.

- ☐ Always has to beat me in games.

- ☐ Has said mean things about me behind my back.

- ☐ Teases me about the way I look.

How many boxes did you check?

0 to 2: This friendship may be worth saving. Talk to your friend using the words "I feel...when you..." Does he or she listen?

3 to 4: This "friend" treats you badly. It's time to take a step back and focus on other friends.

5 to 7: This person is a bully, not a buddy. Steer clear! Turn the page for tips on dealing with bullies.

STANDING UP FOR OTHERS

If you hurt a zombie pigman in Minecraft, what do the other pigmen do? They all come after you! In real life, it's not always easy to stand up for other people. But if enough of you speak up, you can stop bullies in their tracks.

Check off the things you think YOU could do:

☐ Say to the bully, "That's not very funny."

☐ Say to the bully, "You're bullying. Stop it."

☐ Ask the person being bullied, "Are you okay?"

☐ Go stand by the person being bullied.

☐ Say to the person being bullied, "C'mon, let's get out of here."

☐ Invite the person being bullied to hang out with you and your friends.

Practice the words you checked in front of the mirror so that you have them when you need them.

GOOD WORDS ♥♥♥♥♥♥♥♥♥

When you're kind to others, it gives you a boost of confidence, too.

Unscramble the words below for ways to spread kindness.

Laugh at someone's K-J-E-O _____.

L-E-S-M-I _____ at everyone you meet.

Make a D-C-R-A _____ to thank someone for something they did for you.

Help a family member do his or her

H-R-E-C-O-S _____.

Share a K-S-C-N-A _____ with a friend.

C-O-T-P-M-N-M-L-I-E _____ someone on something they do well.

DON'T STRESS

In the Minecraft world as well as your world, there are lots of things that can cause stress. But you don't have to explode when you're feeling stressed. Instead, you can choose to change a thought, feeling, or behavior.

Read about ways to change a thought, feeling, or behavior. Put a check by the ones you might try the next time you're feeling stressed.

Ways to Change a Thought

Say to yourself:

☐ I can do this!

☐ This is not as bad as it seems.

☐ This won't last forever.

Ask yourself:

☐ What do I need?

☐ Who can help me?

☐ What can I learn from this?

Ways to Change a Feeling

Say to yourself:

☐ All feelings are normal.

☐ Feelings are good information.

Try this:

☐ Do something you enjoy.

☐ Talk to someone.

☐ Take a deep breath.

Sometimes I feel trapped in my thoughts or feelings.

Ways to Change a Behavior

Try this:

☐ Take a break.

☐ Walk away.

☐ Speak up.

☐ Smile.

☐ Take a deep breath.

☐ Ask for help.

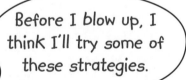

Before I blow up, I think I'll try some of these strategies.

CHANGE IT!

Write about a problem that has caused you some stress. Then write about how you could change a thought, feeling, or behavior. Refer to some of the strategies you checked on the previous page.

MY PROBLEM

How I Can Change My Thoughts

How I Can Change My Feelings

How I Can Change My Behavior

JUST BREATHE

When you're feeling a little stressed, try these breathing exercises.

Breath of Fire

Inhale deeply through your nose.

Then push your breath out through your mouth as you make a *ch, ch, ch, ch* sound.

Repeat.

Dandelion Breath

Inhale slowly through your mouth.

Then exhale slowly, like you are blowing on a dandelion.

Repeat.

Straw Breath

Roll your tongue or use a straw.

Take a big, slow breath in through your tongue or the straw.

Hold it for a moment.

Then breathe out slowly through your nose.

Block Breath

Bring your hands together.

Imagine that you're holding a small diamond block.

Inhale deeply, as you imagine the block growing.

Pause for a moment.

Exhale, as you imagine the block getting smaller.

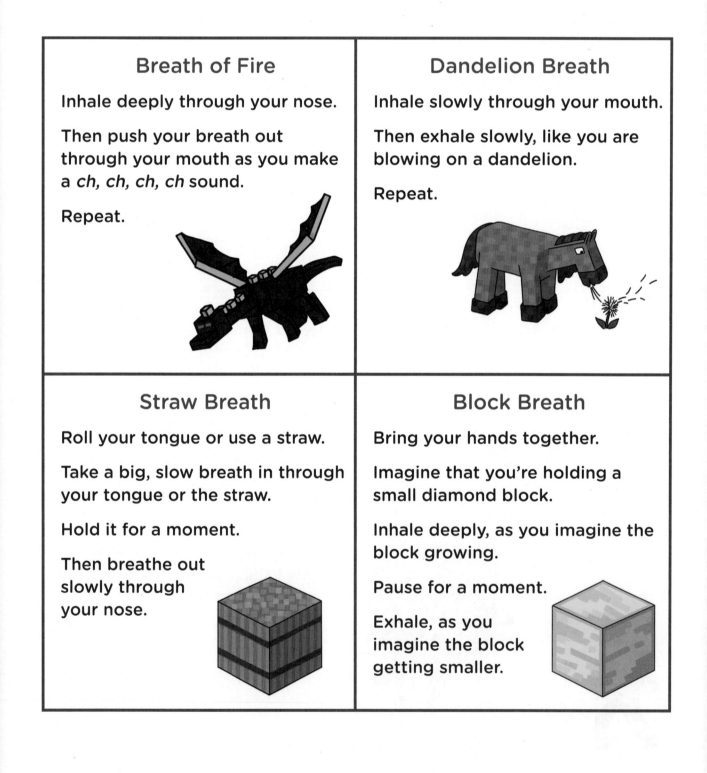

MINE-FUL SENSING

Being mindful calms the mind and the body. It is good for your health. Next time you're feeling stressed, try this mindfulness exercise. Sit quietly and use your senses as you count down.

(5) Look around and locate five things you can see.

(4) Listen. Notice four things you can hear.

(3) Stay seated. Notice three things you can feel.

Can you feel what you're sitting on?

Can you feel the temperature of the room?

Can you feel your hair, your skin, or your clothes?

(2) Inhale deeply. Notice two things you can smell.

Can you smell the scent of your shampoo or soap?

Can you smell something cooking?

Can you smell a pet?

(1) Notice one thing you can taste.

Can you taste what you ate or drank earlier?

Can you taste toothpaste?

MINE-FULNESS IN THE OCEAN

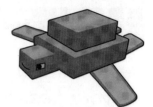

Coloring can be a calming activity for some kids. Being by the ocean or watching fish swim can also calm a busy mind. Color this picture and think about what calms you.

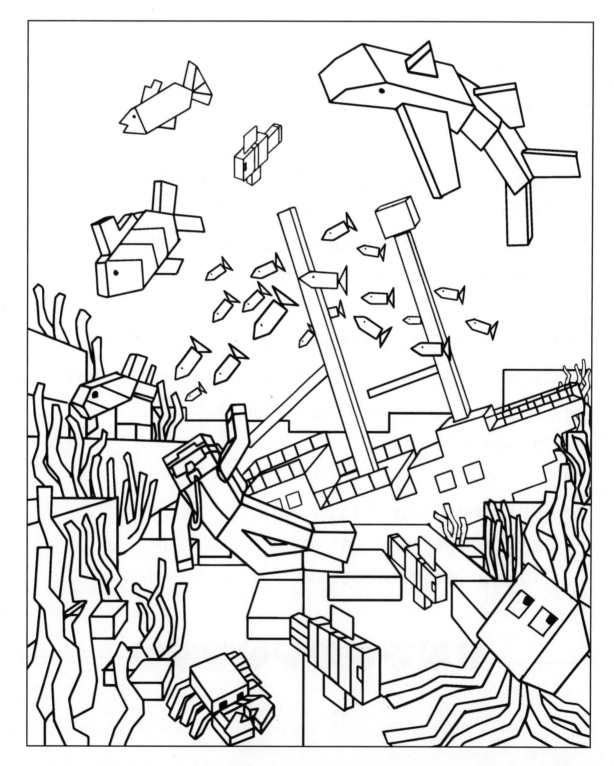

GROW YOUR BRAIN

Did you know that you can grow pathways in your brain to help you learn new things in Minecraft and in school? Follow the path of things the growing brain says to lead you through the maze.

Growing Brain Says:

I can do it!
I love a challenge.
I'll keep trying.
I got this!

Stuck Brain Says:

I can't do it.
This is impossible.
I give up.
I'll never get this.

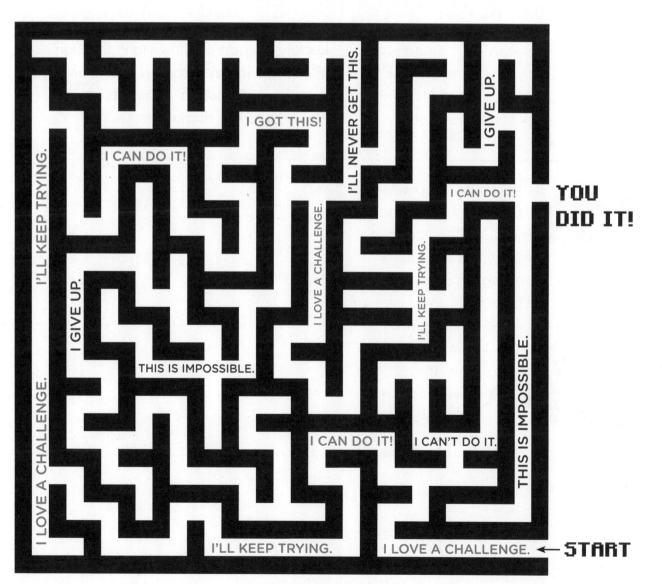

BAD NEWS, GOOD NEWS

It is said that every cloud has a silver lining. That means that even when a situation looks gloomy, there is something that can be appreciated. When you look for the good in a bad situation, you're an optimist. People who look for the good are happier.

Read the bad news. Then write some good news that might come out of the situation. The first one is done for you.
Make up your own bad news and good news for the last one.

BAD NEWS!	GOOD NEWS!
Skeleton shot an arrow at a player, but the arrow hit a tree and now it's heading back toward skeleton.	Luckily, the arrow flew right through skeleton without hitting a bone. Skeleton quickly shot another arrow at the player, causing damage.
Guardians need water to spawn. Unfortunately, the guardian is out of water. It is squeaking loudly and flopping around. Its spikes are sticking out.	
Alex is battling the dragon, but she is losing. The battle is almost done.	

TURN THAT FROWN UPSIDE DOWN

An optimist sees an opportunity in every problem. When thinking about problems, optimists think:

I can figure this out.
I don't understand this *yet*.
There's something to learn from this.

List the things that make you frown. Then turn your frown upside down by changing your thoughts and thinking like an optimist.

Problems	Think Like an Optimist

Some see a weed, but I see a wish.

CHALLENGE ACCEPTED!

Write a problem you have and tell how you will accept or have accepted the challenge!

HOW TO TURN A PROBLEM INTO A CHALLENGE

When something seems hard	THINK	I can learn something new.
When you're not good at something	THINK	I can keep practicing.
When something isn't working	THINK	I can think in a new way.
When something seems impossible	THINK	I can ask for help.

MY PROBLEM	CHALLENGE ACCEPTED!

BOUNCE BACK!

Everyone has a bad day sometimes. When you're feeling sad, bored, or angry, remember you can bounce back by thinking:

Tomorrow will be better.   It's okay. Things happen.   I can ask for help.

My family loves me no matter what.   Things change.   I can do this.

Read the problems that the mobs are having. Then write something they can do to bounce back and improve their mood.

I'm angry. Nothing is going right. First, I lost my parent. Then, I was struck by lightning.	
I'm confused. I don't know how to use this contraption.	
I'm sad because a player trapped me. I'll never get out of here.	
I'm bored because no one will play with me. I even have to eat alone.	

ZOMBIES BOUNCE BACK GAME

Bounce back from a zombie invasion! Cut the Bounce Back Cards at the end of the book (page 355) and place them face down in a pile. Find a friend to play the game with, markers for both of you, and a die.

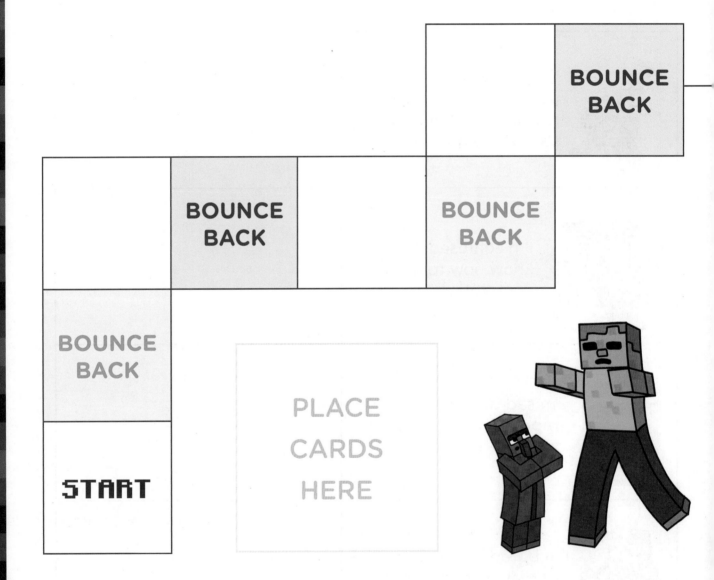

BOUNCE BACK

BOUNCE BACK

BOUNCE BACK

BOUNCE BACK

PLACE CARDS HERE

START

To Play: Have the first player roll the die and move the number of spaces shown on the die. If the player lands on a BOUNCE BACK space, they draw a card and read it aloud. The player must tell a way to bounce back from the event or move back the number of spaces indicated on the card. Players alternate turns until one player reaches the finish.

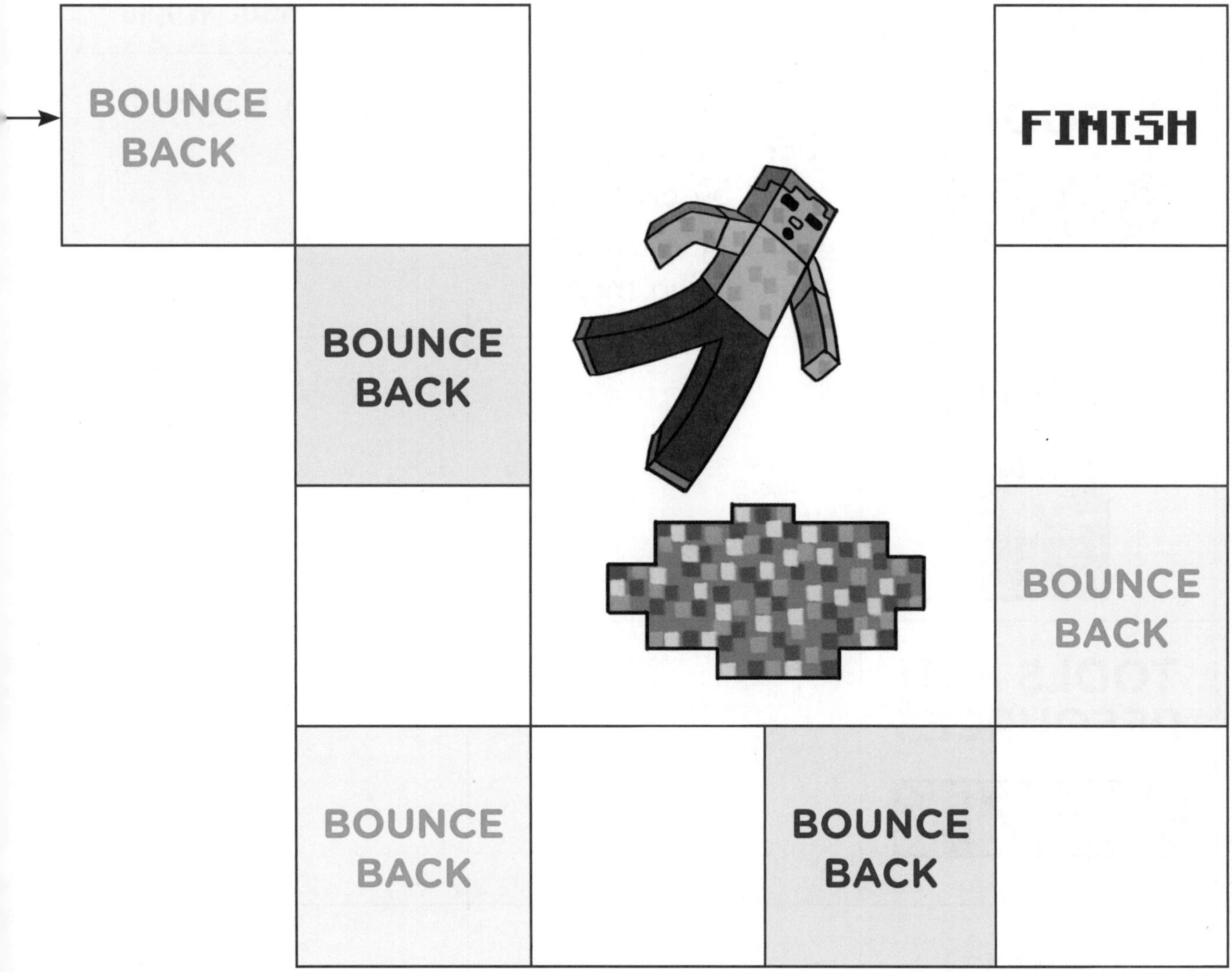

BOUNCE BACK

BOUNCE BACK

BOUNCE BACK

BOUNCE BACK

BOUNCE BACK

FINISH

KNOW YOUR NEEDS

In Minecraft Survival, players eat, build structures, gather tools, and explore. In the real world, people need air, water, food, shelter, and sleep to live. Complete the chart to compare what you need to survive in the Minecraft world and in the real world and how you get what you need. The first Minecraft need (food) is done for you.

When I need…	In Minecraft	In the Real World
FOOD	When my hunger bar is low, I get food by crafting, trading, farming, and killing mobs.	When I'm hungry, I
SHELTER		
TOOLS AND RESOURCES		
HEALTH		

ASK FOR HELP

Everyone needs help sometimes. When you know what you need, think about whom you can ask. If the first person you ask can't help you, ask someone else. Keep asking until you get your needs met. You are worth it!

When You Ask for Help

THINK: Who can help?

ASK: Can you please help me _____?

REMEMBER: Be polite. Use words like *please*, *thank you*, and *excuse me*.

Read the need. Write a sentence asking for help getting the need met.

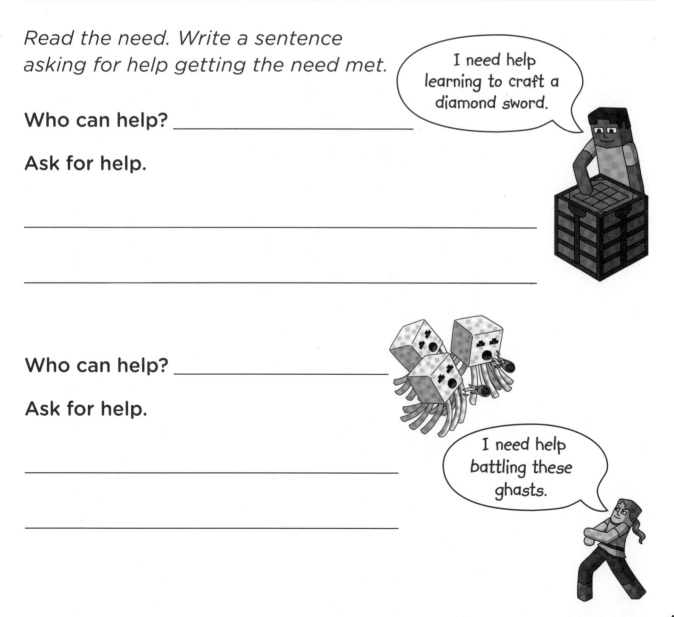

I need help learning to craft a diamond sword.

Who can help? _____

Ask for help.

_____

_____

Who can help? _____

Ask for help.

_____

_____

I need help battling these ghasts.

A NOTE TO MYSELF

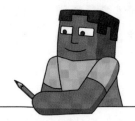

We all make mistakes. We all have things about ourselves that bug us. But just like it's important to be kind to others, it's important to be kind to yourself. Write about a mistake you made or something that you don't like about yourself. Then write a kind note to encourage yourself. Write to yourself like you would write to a good friend with the same problem.

My mistake or something that bugs me about myself is _____

_____

Kind Note to Myself

_____

_____

_____

_____

_____

STEM QUEST CHALLENGES

DRAGON EGG GEODE

Transform an eggshell into a crystal-filled geode using the power of solubility.

Ever wonder what's inside a dragon egg in Minecraft? It's fun to come up with ideas. Maybe the eggs are like **GEODES**, hollow rocks with crystals growing inside. In this activity, you'll make homegrown geodes from eggshells and grow **CRYSTALS** inside using a special **MINERAL SOLUTION** and the properties of **SOLUBILITY**. It takes some time for crystals to form, but it's worth the wait.

INSTRUCTIONS

Day 1

1. Crack the egg as close to the top of the narrow end as possible. Remove the egg yolk and egg white and discard or save for another use.

2. Carefully rinse the eggshell under warm water. Peel off and throw away any small pieces of shell hanging on the edge.

3. Gently peel the inner membrane from the shell. This step is tricky and might take several tries. Having trouble? You can use half of a plastic egg instead.

4. With the paintbrush, cover the inside of the shell and the cracked edges completely with glue.

5. Sprinkle lots of alum powder on the wet glue. Then hold the shell over a paper towel and very gently shake out any extra alum.

6. Allow the egg—cracked side up—to dry overnight on a paper plate. Make sure to wash your hands with soap and water after handling raw eggs.

MATERIALS

- raw egg (or plastic egg half)
- small paintbrush
- white glue
- alum powder (from spice section of grocery store)
- paper towel
- paper plate
- water
- measuring cup
- microwave oven
- purple food coloring
- magnifying glass

Day 2

1. In the microwave, bring 2 cups of water to a boil. Have an adult help you remove the hot water from the microwave.

2. Add 30–40 drops of food coloring to the hot water and stir.

3. Add ¾ cup of alum powder to the hot water. Stir well until the alum is completely dissolved.

4. Let the water and alum mixture cool for 30 minutes.

5. Gently place your eggshell into the mixture, with the cracked side facing up. Allow the shell to soak in mixture for 12–15 hours.

6. Carefully remove the shell and place it cracked side up on a paper towel to dry.

7. Use the magnifying glass to check out your amazing crystals!

WHAT REALLY HAPPENED?

- Crystals appeared as the mixture cooled because of **SOLUBILITY.** That big term simply means the largest amount of something (alum) that can be dissolved in something else (water).

- The solubility of most solids increases with temperature, so more alum could combine with the hot water. But when the mixture cooled, not all the alum could fit into the cooler water and it formed into **CRYSTALS.**

- Natural geodes and crystals can take thousands of years to form. Geodes can be found all over the world, but they are usually found in deserts, volcanic ash beds, or areas with limestone—not surprising now that you know how **TEMPERATURE CHANGES** can help the process.

YOUR TURN TO EXPERIMENT

- Purchase real geode kits and crack them open, according to the directions and with the help of an adult. Every geode is unique and has distinct beauty to discover.

- Create more eggshell geodes of different colors, allowing them to stay in the water-alum mixture longer. You can set up an experiment to compare the weight of the crystals to the length of time they soaked in the mixture. Use the chart on page 47 to record your results. You will need a kitchen scale to measure weight.

DOES THE LENGTH OF SOAKING TIME DETERMINE THE WEIGHT OF THE CRYSTAL?

	Color	Beginning weight	Days of growth	End weight
Crystal 1				
Crystal 2				
Crystal 3				
Crystal 4				
Crystal 5				

FOAMING POTION

Produce an exothermic reaction and a frenzy of bubbles from just a few simple ingredients.

You won't need glowstone dust, magma cream, or blaze powder for this potion. **YEAST** and **HYDROGEN PEROXIDE** are the secret ingredients to create bubbles, a bit of heat, and a **FOAMING EFFECT**. It may be best to take it outside for easier cleanup. For mess control if you're stuck inside, use a cookie sheet or shallow basin. This potion isn't safe to drink, but it's a lot of fun to make and watch.

INSTRUCTIONS

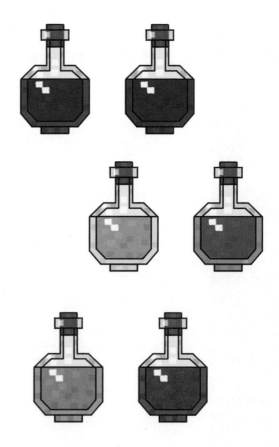

1. Combine the hydrogen peroxide and food coloring in the plastic bottle.

2. Add the dish soap and swish to mix. Touch the side of the bottle and note the warmth of the mixture. Does it feel room temperature, cool, or warm?

3. To a separate bowl, add the warm water and yeast. Mix together until the yeast is dissolved.

4. Using the funnel, add the water-yeast mixture to the bottle. Then watch the foaminess begin!

5. Feel the bottle again or even touch the foam—it's completely safe to touch. Do you notice a change in temperature?

MATERIALS

- 1 bottle 3% hydrogen peroxide solution
- 8 drops food coloring (color of your choice)
- clean 1-liter plastic bottle
- 1 tablespoon liquid dish soap
- small bowl
- 4 tablespoons warm water
- 1 tablespoon active dry yeast
- funnel (optional)

WHAT REALLY HAPPENED?

- ☀ The yeast (which is a tiny living organism used to help bread rise) helped remove the oxygen from the hydrogen peroxide and made tons and tons of tiny **BUBBLES**.

- ☀ The dish soap trapped the oxygen as it was released and made the amazing **FOAM** you saw.

- ☀ Did you notice that the bottle was warmer after the experiment? The chemical reaction that took place is called an **EXOTHERMIC REACTION,** which means that it created heat. This exothermic reaction is completely safe to touch and even rinse down the drain.

YOUR TURN TO EXPERIMENT

- ☀ Try using different dish soaps and different amounts of yeast to find the best recipe for a perfectly foamy potion.

ROCKET REACTION

Launch a miniature rocket using a chemical reaction and Newton's Third Law of Motion.

In Minecraft, **GUNPOWDER** powers firework rockets that create an **EXPLOSION** of colorful fireworks. You can power your own mini rocket and colorful launch with the force of a **CHEMICAL REACTION**. The main rocket "fuel" is a common drugstore item. To have space for the launch and explosion of color, take this project outside.

INSTRUCTIONS

1. Mix the cornstarch with the water in a small bowl.

2. Add the food coloring and stir to combine.

3. Fill the canister or container ⅔ full with the cornstarch solution.

4. Take your project outside.

5. Place the antacid tablet in the cornstarch solution. If it's difficult to fit in, you can break it into smaller pieces.

6. *Quickly* put the cap on the canister or container and turn it upside down.

7. Watch as your rocket explodes!

WHAT REALLY HAPPENED?

※ When you added the antacid to the water, a chemical reaction took place that made **CARBON DIOXIDE,** a gas.

※ As the container started to fill up with carbon dioxide, it put **PRESSURE** on the container. Eventually so much pressure pushed on the inside of the canister that it pushed the cap away.

※ When the cap was pushed down by the gas pressure, the canister blasted up. Sir Isaac Newton, a scientist who studied motion, called this reaction the **THIRD LAW OF MOTION.** It states that for every action, there is an equal and opposite reaction.

* Real rockets use Newton's Third Law of Motion too. As the rocket's fuel combines with oxygen, it produces gases that are directed out the rear of the rocket to propel it up.

YOUR TURN TO EXPERIMENT

* Add different amounts of antacid tablets. Does the rocket fly higher? Does the reaction take place more quickly?

* Try using other containers (no glass or metal) to make a rocket. Add fins and a nose as extra touches, just like a real rocket. Does the flight pattern change?

* Attempt to control the direction of the rocket. In Minecraft, you can position firework rockets to travel in different directions by launching them under flowing water. Try laying your rocket on its side or changing the angle by propping it against a small stone.

MATERIALS

* ½ cup cornstarch
* ½ cup water
* small bowl
* 6–8 drops of red food coloring
* empty film canister or clean, empty glue stick container
* 1 antacid tablet (such as Alka-Seltzer)

PIXEL POWER

Ever wonder how the images in Minecraft are created? Computers draw using **PIXELS,** which are tiny points of color. So how do the pixels know where to appear? That's up to the **PROGRAMMER.** In this activity, *you* are the programmer who will create a mystery Minecraft image based on **GRIDS AND COORDINATES.**

INSTRUCTIONS

A grid can be used to imagine the way pixels are stored in the computer's memory. Coordinates on the grid are used to give the location of each pixel, starting with the upper left corner, then the one to the right, until they work their way over to the right edge of the grid. Then the next row of pixels is loaded on the next line down.

For example, if you wanted to put a red dot in the middle of the graph below, you would give the computer these coordinates:

```
(3, 3 red)
```

The first number tells the computer to go 3 pixels to the right (starting at the upper left-hand-corner of the screen).

The second number tells the computer to drop 3 squares down. The word "red" tells the computer to fill in that pixel with the color red.

MATERIALS

◆ Colored pencils in the following colors: dark green, light green, dark brown, medium brown, light brown, dark blue, light blue

Now *you* be the computer. Look at the pairs of coordinates to draw a smiley face on this little screen. The first pixel is drawn for you: 2 to the right, 2 down, black.

See if you can use the coordinates to draw the rest.

(2, 2 black)	(2, 5 black) ■
(5, 2 black) ■	(5, 5 black) ■
(1, 4 black) ■	(3, 6 black) ■
(6, 4 black) ■	(4, 6 black) ■

0	1	2	3	4	5	6
1						
2		■				
3						
4						
5						
6						

YOUR TURN TO EXPERIMENT

Now it's time to take your learning about pixels and computer graphics coordinate systems to the next level! Use the coordinates on page 54 to create a mystery image. To make this activity a little easier, the coordinates are written on a table with all of the coordinates for the different colors separated on their own table. What Minecraft image did you create by following the coordinates? Check your answer on page 343.

	Across	Down
Dark Green	17	3
Dark Green	18	3
Dark Green	19	3
Dark Green	16	4
Dark Green	19	4
Dark Green	15	5
Dark Green	19	5
Dark Green	14	6
Dark Green	18	6
Dark Green	13	7
Dark Green	17	7
Dark Green	12	8
Dark Green	16	8
Dark Green	6	9
Dark Green	7	9
Dark Green	11	9
Dark Green	15	9
Dark Green	6	10
Dark Green	8	10
Dark Green	10	10
Dark Green	14	10
Dark Green	7	11
Dark Green	9	11
Dark Green	13	11
Dark Green	7	12
Dark Green	9	12
Dark Green	12	12
Dark Green	8	13
Dark Green	10	13
Dark Green	11	13
Dark Green	9	14
Dark Green	12	14
Dark Green	10	15

	Across	Down
Dark Green	11	15
Dark Green	13	15
Dark Green	4	16
Dark Green	5	16
Dark Green	12	16
Dark Green	13	16
Dark Green	4	17
Dark Green	6	17
Dark Green	4	18
Dark Green	5	18
Dark Green	6	18
Light Green	7	10
Light Green	8	11
Light Green	8	12
Light Green	9	13
Light Green	10	14
Light Green	11	14
Light Green	12	15
Light Green	5	17
Dark Brown	7	14
Dark Brown	6	15
Dark Brown	8	15
Dark Brown	7	16
Med Brown	6	15
Med Brown	5	16

	Across	Down
Light Blue	17	4
Light Blue	16	5
Light Blue	18	5
Light Blue	15	6
Light Blue	17	6
Light Blue	14	7
Light Blue	16	7
Light Blue	13	8
Light Blue	15	8
Light Blue	12	9
Light Blue	14	9
Light Blue	11	10
Light Blue	13	10
Light Blue	10	11
Light Blue	12	11
Light Blue	11	12
Dark Blue	18	4
Dark Blue	17	5
Dark Blue	16	6
Dark Blue	15	7
Dark Blue	14	8
Dark Blue	13	9
Dark Blue	12	10
Dark Blue	11	11
Dark Blue	10	12

	0	1	2	3	4	5	6	7	8	9	10	11	12	13	14	15	16	17	18	19	20
1																					
2																					
3																					
4																					
5																					
6																					
7																					
8																					
9																					
10																					
11																					
12																					
13																					
14																					
15																					
16																					
17																					
18																					
19																					
20																					

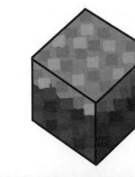

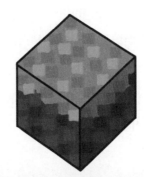

SLIME BLOCK POLYMER

Discover how a basic school supply can create a polymer with fun, bouncy properties.

You've played with bouncy balls . . . but what about bouncing cubes? You can create a rubbery **POLYMER** (a large molecule made of repeating chains of smaller chemical units) that will have some bounce in just about any shape. Adding **GLUE** to a solution of **BORAX** (a mineral often used as a laundry powder) creates the chemical reaction for the effect you want. Have fun making your own slime block that bounces randomly, just like the slime blocks that spawn deep underground in Minecraft.

INSTRUCTIONS

1. In the measuring cup, add the water and borax. Stir the mixture until the borax is completely dissolved. (You may need to microwave the solution for 10–20 seconds to help it dissolve. Be sure to check with an adult before using.)

2. Allow the mixture to cool to room temperature, about 30 minutes.

3. Add the glue to the cooled borax solution. (Add more or less glue depending on how large you want your slime block to be.)

4. With your fingers, squish the glue in the borax solution until it is no longer sticky. You will feel the glue start to harden and stick together.

5. Remove the glue from the measuring cup and continue smooshing it together for a few more seconds until it forms a glob that is starting to become hard.

6. Place the glue glob in a square section of the ice cube tray and smoosh it into the corners and bottom of the square.

7. Allow the glue to harden in the ice cube tray for at least 1 hour. (For best results, allow 12–24 hours for hardening.) Your slime block is ready

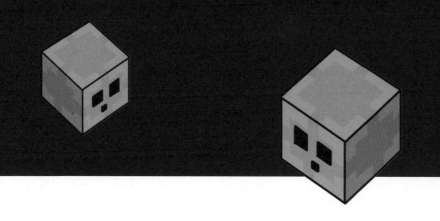

MATERIALS

- liquid measuring cup
- ½ cup hot water
- 1 tablespoon borax (found in the laundry section of the store)
- 1–2 tablespoons clear green glitter school glue
- ice cube tray

to bounce once it has hardened and you can no longer feel moisture on the outside. Store your cube in an airtight container between uses so it doesn't dry out.

WHAT REALLY HAPPENED?

* Adding glue to a water/borax solution caused a **CHEMICAL REACTION** between the glue molecules and the borax molecules. When the glue molecules reacted with the borax, a polymer was made.

* **POLYMERS** are large molecules made of repeating chains of smaller chemical units.

* Polymers are different depending on what types of **CHAINS** are linked together. The polymer you made is rubbery, like the polymer used to make bouncy balls. In this kind of polymer, the chains are flexible. Some polymers are sticky, like silly putty; other polymers can be hard, like a skateboard.

YOUR TURN TO EXPERIMENT

* Try making different sizes of slime block. You will need to make a fresh batch of borax solution each time. Vary the amount of glue you add to make the cubes smaller or larger. When they are all hard and dry, test them in the ultimate bounce off! Which one bounces the highest? Which one bounces the most times?

FLUORESCING GLOWSTONE

Transform milk into plastic, then add a special ingredient to make it glow.

Glowstones are brightly glowing blocks found in the Nether. They can be used as a **LIGHT SOURCE** or to make redstone lamps. In this activity, you can make your own glowstone by turning milk into plastic and adding the ink from a highlighter to make it **FLUORESCE** (you will need a black light to see the fluorescence).

INSTRUCTIONS

1. Pour the milk into the glass measuring cup. Microwave for 2 minutes. Have an adult help remove the milk from the microwave; it will be hot.

2. In a separate bowl, mix the white vinegar with the food coloring.

3. Remove the ink from the highlighter and add the ink to the bowl containing the vinegar and food coloring. (Set the highlighter tip aside for later use in this activity.)

4. Add the colored vinegar to the hot milk and stir. The milk will curdle and form clumps.

5. Strain the milk through the cloth, collecting the clumps in the cloth. Discard the liquid. Use the rubber band to tie off the cloth and make a pouch containing the milk clumps. Allow to cool for 20–30 minutes.

6. When the milk clumps are cool enough to handle, unwrap the pouch and smoosh the clumps together until you can form a shape. This is your milk "plastic."

7. Press the milk plastic into a section in an ice cube tray. Allow the plastic to harden for 30–60 minutes.

8. Remove the milk plastic after it has hardened.

9. Use the highlighter tip to add spots to the glowstone.

10. In a dark room lit with the black light, check out your glowstone.

WHAT REALLY HAPPENED?

✳ Milk contains protein molecules called casein. Adding vinegar to hot milk caused the casein molecules to unfold and create long chains called a polymer. This polymer can be molded and shaped, which makes it a plastic. Buttons in the nineteenth century were made out of this type of plastic, known as **CASEIN PLASTIC.**

✳ Black lights emit **ULTRAVIOLET (UV) LIGHT,** which we cannot see. Fluorescence is light given off by certain substances when they absorb UV light. First these substances absorb energy, and then they give off the light.

YOUR TURN TO EXPERIMENT

✳ Try making this plastic with milk containing other percentages of fat, such as 1%, 2%, whipping cream, or half-and-half. What happens?

✳ Investigate other objects you can create using casein plastic.

✳ Do some research to see which animals have the ability of biofluorescence and how this adaptation helps them survive in their habitat.

TIME

30 minutes

MATERIALS

◆ 1 cup whole milk

◆ glass measuring cup

◆ microwave

◆ small bowl

◆ 4 teaspoons white vinegar

◆ 4 drops green food coloring and 2 drops brown food coloring

◆ highlighter with liquid ink

◆ scrap of fabric or cheesecloth

◆ rubber band

◆ ice cube tray

◆ black light

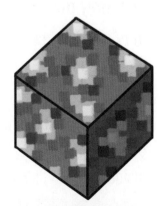

BEACON LUMINESCENCE

Observe how light is just a snap away with a chemical reaction that results in luminescence.

Beacons are one of the most powerful things you can create in Minecraft. It is difficult to obtain the resources to build them, but they are worth it! In this demonstration, you will examine the **CHEMISTRY** behind a much easier and more common way to create light: glow sticks. Although nowadays we use glow sticks for fun, they were first invented to be used as **EMERGENCY LIGHT SOURCES** for the US Navy in 1973. Since they are nonflammable and nonsparking, they are safe for use immediately after a catastrophic event. Glow sticks use a **CHEMICAL REACTION** that results in a phenomenon called **LUMINESCENCE.** You'll observe the results of this demonstration best in near or complete darkness.

 This activity involves using sharp knives and breaking glass, and therefore it should be conducted by an adult as a demonstration for children to watch.

INSTRUCTIONS

1. Put on rubber gloves and safety glasses. Ask children to stand several feet away from your work area.

2. Very carefully, cut off the tip of a glow stick.

3. Pour the contents of the glow stick into a glass or plastic cup, taking care to gently remove the small glass cylinder inside the glow stick.

4. Turn off or dim the lights.

5. While wearing rubber gloves, break the glass cylinder over the cup so that the contents pour into the cup. Watch what happens!

MATERIALS

- rubber gloves
- safety glasses
- glow stick
- sharp knife and cutting board or sharp scissors
- small glass or clear plastic cup

WHAT REALLY HAPPENED?

✳ Did you know that glow sticks use a chemical reaction to make light? Glow sticks contain two separate compartments with different chemicals. The outer compartment is plastic, while the inner compartment is made of glass. When you bend the glow stick to activate it, you are breaking a glass cylinder to release the chemical in the inner compartment. When the chemical in the inner glass cylinder comes in contact with the chemical in the outer plastic cylinder, a chemical reaction takes place.

✳ Glow sticks produce light through **CHEMILUMINESCENCE,** which produces light without making any heat.

✳ Glow sticks have many qualities that make them useful in extreme conditions. They can tolerate high pressures, they are waterproof and weatherproof, they are visible for up to a mile in optimal conditions, and they are nonflammable and nonsparking.

YOUR TURN TO EXPERIMENT

✳ Go hot or cold. Chemical reactions are affected by temperature. What would happen if you changed the temperature of the glow sticks before the chemicals combine? Put one glow stick in ice-cold water and another glow stick in very hot water for a few minutes and then repeat the experiment. Do both glow sticks glow as brightly?

✳ Mix up colors. What happens when you combine different colors of glow sticks?

COLOR-CHANGING PH POTIONS

Watch this magical potion change color based on pH levels.

Minecraft has many magical potions, but none is as pretty or as amazing as the one you will create in this activity. This potion changes its color based on the type of **SOLUTION** it is mixed with. It can be used to test various household solutions for **ACIDITY.**

INSTRUCTIONS

1. Have an adult cut half of a red cabbage into small pieces.

2. Place the pieces of cabbage in a large bowl.

3. Have an adult help with boiling enough water to cover the cabbage. Pour the boiling water over the cabbage pieces. Allow the cabbage to sit in the hot water for 10 minutes.

4. Pour the cabbage water through the strainer into a second bowl. You can discard the cabbage.

5. Dilute the cabbage water with cold water until it's slightly transparent but still purple.

6. While you wait for the cabbage juice to cool, label each of 6 glasses and add ¼–⅓ cup of one of the following:
   - water
   - baking soda solution
   - vinegar
   - ammonia
   - dish soap
   - lemon juice

7. Test the pH of each liquid and record the results in the table on page 64. Follow the directions on the pH indicator strip container. Alternatively, use the internet to research the pH of the liquids and record the information in the table.

MATERIALS

- ½ red cabbage
- knife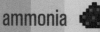
- cutting board
- 2 large bowls
- boiling water
- strainer
- cold water
- 12 small glasses or clear plastic cups
- 2 tablespoons baking soda mixed with water until thin
- vinegar
- ammonia
- liquid dish soap
- lemon juice
- pH test strips (optional) or internet for research
- blue, green, purple, and pink colored pencils

8. Either using the information included with the pH test strips, or the internet, indicate (in the table) if each liquid is an acid or a base.

9. Pour the cabbage juice into the remaining 6 glasses or cups, filling each about ¾ full. Label the glasses with the same labels used in Step 6.

10. Red cabbage juice changes color when mixed with an acid or a base. Acids turn PINK and bases turn BLUE or GREEN. Neutral solutions remain PURPLE.

11. Before you test the liquids with the cabbage juice, make a prediction about which color each liquid will become. Use your colored pencils to shade in the table below based on your predictions.

12. Prepare to be amazed! One at a time, pour each solution into the corresponding cup of cabbage juice.

13. Shade in the table with the colors that appeared when you added the cabbage juice. Were your predictions correct?

Solution	pH	Acid or Base?	Predicted Color	Actual Color
Water				
Baking soda				
Vinegar				
Ammonia				
Dish soap				
Lemon juice				

WHAT REALLY HAPPENED?

❊ Some substances can be classified as either an acid or a base. **ACIDS AND BASES** are opposites. Acids taste sour and feel sticky, and their smell can burn the nose. Vinegar is an example of an acid that is safe to taste. Bases taste bitter, feel slippery, and usually do not have a smell. Baking soda is an example of a base that is safe to taste. *Never taste, touch, or smell unknown substances without permission from an adult.*

❊ Scientists measure how strong an acid or a base is using a **pH SCALE,** which goes from 0–14. Acids have a low pH, while bases have a high pH. Water is referred to as neutral, because it is neither acidic or basic. Water's pH is 7.

❊ As you observed, cabbage juice turns red when it mixes with something acidic, and it turns green or blue when it mixes with something basic. Red cabbage juice is called an **INDICATOR** because it shows us if the solution is an acid or a base.

❊ Red cabbage juice contains a pigment called anthocyanin, which changes color when mixed with an acid or base.

YOUR TURN TO EXPERIMENT

✳ Have an adult help you find other liquids that can safely be tested. Your home is full of solutions that can be tested using red cabbage juice. Make a new data table and continue investigating.

✳ Make your own pH test strips. Use the other half of the cabbage to make a concentrated cabbage juice (follow Steps 1–4 on page 62). Soak coffee filter paper in cabbage juice and then remove the paper and hang it to dry. Cut the dried paper into strips and use it to test various liquids. If the paper turns red, the liquid is acidic. If the paper turns green, the liquid is a base. If it stays purple, the liquid is probably neutral.

LLAMA LAB

Test your saliva for enzymes that help your body in the process of digesting food.

Llamas are famous for their nasty habit of spitting when they are annoyed or angry. Even in Minecraft, llamas spit. You will need to pretend to be a llama in this activity as you collect some of your saliva. Your mission: to discover how **DIGESTION** begins in the mouth with **CHEMICAL REACTIONS** caused by molecules called **ENZYMES**. You will be testing for an enzyme called **SALIVARY AMYLASE**. Salivary amylase is a common enzyme found in our mouths that helps us break down starch. **STARCH** is a molecule found in plants and common in many foods we eat, including anything made with flour.

INSTRUCTIONS

1. Combine the iodine and ¼ cup water in a glass cup or jar.

2. Put the flour into a mug. Have an adult help you fill the mug with boiling water. Stir and allow to cool to room temperature, about 20–30 minutes.

3. Label your test tubes as follows:
   - Saliva
   - Control
   - 20 minutes
   - 40 minutes
   - 60 minutes

TIME

2 hours

MATERIALS

- ¼ cup iodine
- ¼ cup water + more to boil
- measuring cup
- glass cup or jar
- 1 teaspoon flour
- mug
- 5 test tubes or small containers
- boiling water
- saliva
- eyedropper
- timer

4. Add 1–2 teaspoons of the flour solution to all of the test tubes except the one labeled "saliva."

5. Add 1–2 drops of the iodine-water solution to the test tube labeled "control." The iodine should have turned to a blue-black color or brown. This shows that the solution contains starch.

6. Spit several times into the test tube labeled "saliva." You will need about 2 tablespoons of saliva.

7. Add a few drops of the saliva to the test tube labeled "60 minutes." Set the timer for 20 minutes.

8. When 20 minutes has passed, add a few drops of the saliva to the test tube labeled "40 minutes." Set the timer for 20 minutes.

9. When another 20 minutes has passed (a total of 40 minutes since you started timing), add a few drops of the saliva to the test tube labeled "20 minutes." Set the timer for 20 minutes.

10. During the past 60 minutes, the saliva you added to the "60 minutes" test tube has been very busy "eating" starch in the flour solution. You can now test each solution to find out if there is any starch remaining in the flour solution.

11. Add a few drops of the iodine-water solution to each the test tubes labeled with the 3 different times.

12. Compare the color of the solution in the test tubes with the control. Remember, you did not add any saliva to the control test tube. The test tubes with the darkest colors indicate that there is still starch remaining. The test tubes with the lightest colors indicate that there is less starch remaining.

WHAT REALLY HAPPENED?

❈ The first step of **DIGESTION** begins in the mouth. We chew food into smaller pieces, and our saliva begins to break molecules apart.

❈ Salivary amylase is an enzyme in human saliva that breaks down starch. **ENZYMES** are molecules that help chemical reactions take place more quickly.

IODINE is a chemical commonly used to disinfect wounds. It can also be used to test for the presence of starch. When iodine comes in contact with starch, it turns a bluish-black color.

YOUR TURN TO EXPERIMENT

Leave your test tubes to sit out for several hours or overnight and observe what happens as time elapses. You should notice that eventually all the samples, except the control, are the same color. That shows that the enzymes in your saliva broke down all the starch in the test tube.

Investigate what foods contain starch. You can make a solution by crushing food and dissolving it in water. Use a drop or two of iodine to test the solutions for starch.

CHARGED CREEPER DETECTOR

Make an instrument called an electroscope to detect electric charges.

A charged creeper is created when lightning strikes near a normal creeper. Charged creepers have a blue aura surrounding them, making them easy to spot. But wouldn't it be nice to know if a charged creeper is sneaking up on you? In this activity, you will make an **ELECTROSCOPE**, which detects **ELECTRIC FORCES** in an object. If you could build an electroscope in Minecraft, you would be safer from charged creepers.

INSTRUCTIONS

1. Use the opening of the mason jar as a pattern to draw a circle on the cardboard. Cut out the circle.

2. Use the pin to make a hole in the center of the cardboard.

3. Cut a 3-inch piece of coffee stirrer straw and insert it into the opening of the cardboard circle.

4. Insert the copper wire into the straw so that it extends approximately 3 inches below the cardboard.

5. Bend the end of the copper wire into a hook.

MATERIALS

- wide-mouth mason jar
- thin cardboard (a cereal box works well)
- pin
- coffee stirrer straw
- scissors
- 12-inch copper wire
- 3-inch square of aluminum foil
- electrical tape
- green balloon
- black permanent marker

6. Fold the aluminum foil in half.

7. Cut a teardrop shape out of the aluminum foil. Try to make the shape use as much of the foil as possible. Poke a hole in the narrow pointed side.

8. Unfold the aluminum foil to reveal two identical shapes with holes in the tops.

9. Hang the foil pieces from the hook on the copper wire. Carefully smooth the foil pieces together.

10. Insert the wire with the foil pieces into the jar. Use electrical tape to secure the cardboard circle to the top of the jar.

11. Twist the copper wire that's sticking out of the jar into a flat spiral shape (see the photo on page 71). Bend the spiral to one side.

12. Inflate the balloon and draw a charged creeper using the permanent marker.

13. Vigorously rub the inflated balloon on your hair for at least 30 seconds.

14. Bring the balloon close to (but not touching) the copper spiral and carefully watch the two pieces of aluminum hanging from the copper hook. What happens?

WHAT REALLY HAPPENED?

❋ To understand this activity, you need to understand a little bit about electrons. Atoms have two types of charged particles: **PROTONS AND ELECTRONS.** Protons are positively charged, and electrons are negatively charged. Positive and negative charges attract each other, like the opposite sides of a magnet. When objects with the same charge come in contact with each other, they repel. Playing with magnets is a helpful way to understand how charges interact. If you bring the negative side of a magnet toward the negative side of another magnet, they will push away from each other. The same is true with electrons. If two objects are negatively charged with electrons, they will repel each other.

When you rubbed the balloon on your hair, the balloon became charged with electrons, causing **STATIC ELECTRICITY.** Objects with static have a buildup of electrons on their surface.

As you brought the charged balloon creeper near the copper coil on the electroscope, the electrons from the balloon moved to the copper coil and down to the aluminum foil. When they reached the aluminum foil, the two pieces of foil moved away from each other because they had the same **CHARGE.**

YOUR TURN TO EXPERIMENT

Try charging different objects with static electricity. You can rub them on a piece of foam instead of your hair, if you prefer. Here are some ideas to try charging: comb, metal ruler, plastic wrap, tissue paper, copper, wool, silk. Use the electroscope to test them for a charge.

OBSIDIAN FORMATION

Create your own volcano simulation to see how lava flows and hardens—while recycling old crayons.

Minecrafters use **OBSIDIAN** to build explosion-resistant structures or to create a Nether portal frame. In Minecraft, the resource occurs naturally where underwater springs flow onto lava. In our natural world, obsidian forms when **MOLTEN ROCK** cools quickly. Here, you will create your own model volcano with flowing **LAVA** from melted crayons, which cool into simulated obsidian.

INSTRUCTIONS

1. Stack both pieces of foil over the thin end of a large funnel. Press the foil against the outside of the funnel to create a volcano shape that extends past the bottom of the funnel.

2. Remove the funnel from the foil volcano. Make an indentation about the size of a golf ball on the top of the volcano cone to hold the crayon pieces. You will need one side of the indentation to be lower than the other side. This will allow the melted crayon lava to flow in a controlled pathway down the side of the aluminum volcano.

3. On the side that is lower, use your fingernail or a pen cap to make indented lines from the top of the volcano downward, to resemble streams. This will provide a path for the melted crayons to run down the side of the foil volcano.

4. Peel several crayon pieces and place them in the top of the volcano.

5. Place the baking dish on the table or countertop. Group the tea light candles toward the center of the dish. Place the cooling rack over the baking dish and the candles.

MATERIALS

- 2 pieces (each 2 feet long) heavy duty aluminum foil
- large funnel
- old crayon pieces
- glass baking dish
- 10 tea light candles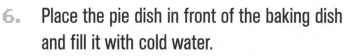
- metal cooling rack (such as one used when baking cookies)
- glass pie dish
- water
- wax paper

6. Place the pie dish in front of the baking dish and fill it with cold water.

7. Have an adult help you light the tea candles.

8. Position the aluminum volcano, with the crayons, on top of the cooling rack so that it is positioned over the lit candles. The bottom of the volcano should sit slightly over the pie plate so that the crayon wax will easily flow directly into the cold water.

9. Check that the paths you made from the top of the volcano lead down the side and over the pie dish. Also be certain that the volcano is positioned so that the lower side containing the crayons is toward the pie dish. The idea is for the crayons to melt and flow out of the indentation, down the paths and into the water.

10. Wait patiently and watch as the crayon rocks melt and the wax lava flows down the side of the aluminum volcano.

11. Allow the lava to flow into the water and harden. When you are done melting the crayon rocks, allow the lava to cool in the water for approximately 60 minutes, then remove it to dry on wax paper.

12. Look carefully at the crayon model of obsidian you created next to images of real hardened lava. How does it compare?

WHAT REALLY HAPPENED?

* When a volcano erupts, it releases hot molten rock called **LAVA**. When lava (real or crayon!) flows into water, it quickly cools and hardens.

* After the lava hardens, it is called **IGNEOUS ROCK.** There are three major types of rocks: metamorphic, igneous, and sedimentary.

* **OBSIDIAN** is a naturally occurring igneous rock that forms when molten rock cools quickly.

YOUR TURN TO EXPERIMENT

* Start a rock collection. There are many resources on the internet for identifying rocks.

* Examine rocks with a magnifying glass to check out the small particles that make up many rocks, such as sedimentary rock.

COLORFUL CRYSTAL CAVE

Grow delicate crystals suspended in colorful displays-evaporation is part of the magic.

Whether it's a diamond, emerald, lapis, prismarine, or end crystal, **CRYSTALS** and **GEMS** mined in Minecraft are valuable. They can be used to create tools, structures, and products, or they can be traded with villagers. Crystals have been admired for thousands of years and used as jewelry, decoration, or in tools. In this activity, you will grow colorful crystals in a cave made of charcoal and sponges with the help of **EVAPORATION** and **COLLOIDAL SUSPENSION.**

INSTRUCTIONS

1. Create a cave by arranging the charcoal briquettes together on the plate. Use 3 sponges to create the sides and back of the cave and lay 1 sponge over the top to create a roof.

2. Sprinkle water on the briquettes and sponges until they are moist.

3. Add the food coloring over the charcoal and sponges. The crystals will only pick up color on the areas that have food coloring. Areas without food coloring will be white.

4. Combine 3 tablespoons of salt, 3 tablespoons of ammonia, and 6 tablespoons of bluing in a jar or dish. Stir until the salt is dissolved.

5. Use the turkey baster to apply the ammonia mixture over the charcoals and sponges until all the areas are saturated. Save any remaining ammonia mixture for later use (see Step 8) in a covered plastic or glass container.

6. Sprinkle 2 more tablespoons of salt on the charcoals and sponges.

7. Allow the crystals to grow undisturbed for 2 or 3 days.

8. Add more ammonia mixture to the cave. Try to avoid applying the solution directly onto the crystals.

WHAT REALLY HAPPENED?

※ This crystal cave was formed by the salt after the water evaporated. The ammonia helped speed up that **EVAPORATION** process. As the water evaporated, the salt formed crystals using the particles in the bluing liquid as "seeds" for growth. Bluing fluid has tiny particles that won't dissolve but are suspended in the liquid; this is called a **COLLOIDAL SUSPENSION.**

YOUR TURN TO EXPERIMENT

※ Try using other materials as the bottom layer (often called the substrate) for growing these crystals. Cardboard or pieces of terra cotta pots may work well. You can even cut cardboard or sponges into different shapes and add colors in certain areas to create artwork.

MATERIALS

- charcoal briquettes (at least 12)
- glass or plastic plate
- 4 cleaning sponges
- water
- food coloring
- 5 tablespoons salt (divided into 3 tablespoons and 2 tablespoons)
- 3 tablespoons ammonia
- 6 tablespoons laundry bluing
- turkey baster
- jar or dish with a lid

TURTLE SHELL SCUBA

Discover if water breathing is really possible—and learn about volume, vacuums, and water displacement.

Wearing a turtle shell gives Minecraft players the ability to breathe underwater for 10 seconds. Is this **"WATER BREATHING"** possible in real life? Discover for yourself by making a model turtle shell and conducting your own underwater experiments.

INSTRUCTIONS

Part 1: Is it possible to trap air underwater?

1. Fill the bowl with water.

2. Cut a piece of green construction paper slightly larger than the bottom of the plastic container. Decorate the paper to look like a turtle shell.

3. Push the construction paper shell into the bottom inside of the plastic container so that you can see the turtle shell drawing when the container is upside down—just like in the top photo on page 81.

4. **Make a prediction:** What will happen if you turn the container upside down and place it on top of the water? Will the paper stay dry or get wet?

5. Turn the container upside down and place it on top of the water.

6. Observe what happens. Was your prediction correct?

Part 2: Is "water breathing" possible?

1. Leave your model turtle shell floating on top of the water.

2. Bend the straw into a J shape.

3. Hold your finger over the opening of the long end of the straw. Don't remove your finger until after Step 4.

4. Place the short end of the straw under the plastic container so that the tip is in the trapped air.

MATERIALS

- large bowl (or aquarium) of clean water
- green construction paper
- small, square plastic container
- black marker
- bendable straw

5. Remove your finger from the end of the straw and blow a small breath through the straw to remove any water that might have become attached at the other end.

6. **Make a prediction:** What will happen if you breathe through the straw?

7. Take in a breath through the straw.

8. Observe what happens. Was your prediction correct?

Part 3: Can you put air back into the container without lifting it?

1. Leave the model turtle shell upside down, filled with water.

2. **Make a prediction:** What will happen if you blow bubbles under the turtle shell?

3. Place the straw so that the tip of the short end is under the turtle shell.

4. Blow bubbles through the straw, underneath the turtle shell.

5. Observe what happens. Was your prediction correct?

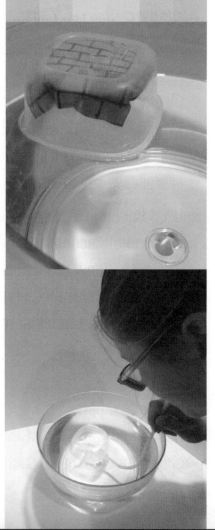

WHAT REALLY HAPPENED?

⁂ When you placed the model turtle shell upside down in the water, the green paper did not get wet. The plastic container did not fill with water, because it was already filled with air. **AIR TAKES UP SPACE,** just like tables, blocks, and everything else that surrounds you. Because water and air cannot occupy the same space at the same time, water cannot flow into the container when air is already trapped inside.

⁂ In the second part of the activity, you used the straw to remove the air from inside the model turtle shell. When the air was sucked out, it created a **VACUUM,** or an empty space. The empty space was immediately taken up by water that rushed into the plastic container and wet the green construction paper.

⁂ In the third part of the activity, bubbles floated up to the top of the model turtle shell. The air bubbles pushed the water out of the shell. This is called **WATER DISPLACEMENT.** Water is displaced, or moved out of the way, to make room for the air. When enough bubbles were blown into the turtle shell, the shell started to float.

⁂ SCUBA is the abbreviation for Self Contained Underwater Breathing Apparatus. SCUBA equipment allows underwater breathing, but not in the same way as a Minecraft turtle shell. SCUBA divers use tanks filled with compressed air to breathe.

YOUR TURN TO EXPERIMENT

⁂ Use water displacement to find an object's volume, the amount of space that it takes up. Fill a measuring cup with water to the ½ cup line. Drop an object into the water and read the new water level. Next, subtract the old volume (½ cup) from the new volume. The answer is equal to the volume of the object.

MAGICAL MAGNETIC GHAST

Use the amazing powers of magnetism to mysteriously move a ghast.

Huge and floating, with scary red eyes, ghasts shoot explosive fireballs at Minecraft players. Our ghast won't have you running for cover, but it will certainly amaze your friends. Use the powers of **MAGNETISM** to magically move your ghast.

INSTRUCTIONS

1. Carefully insert the small magnet into the balloon.

2. Inflate the balloon and tie the end.

3. Using the marker, draw ghast eyes and a mouth (they are typically closed).

4. Place the balloon ghast on top of the cardboard.

5. While holding the cardboard with one hand, hold the larger magnet under the cardboard with the other hand.

6. Move the larger magnet around under the cardboard. The ghast should magically move on top of the cardboard.

WHAT REALLY HAPPENED?

* Magnets have two ends, called **POLES.** One pole is called a north (or north-seeking) pole, and the other is called a south (or south-seeking) pole.

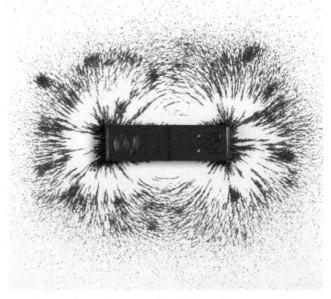

TIME

10 minutes

MATERIALS

- small magnet
- white balloon
- black permanent marker
- thin piece of cardboard (ex: the back of a legal pad)
- large magnet

❄ Opposites attract. The north pole on one magnet is attracted to the south pole of another magnet. North poles repel each other, as do south poles.

❄ A **MAGNETIC FIELD** is an invisible area of magnetism around a magnet.

YOUR TURN TO EXPERIMENT

❄ Create a magnet maze using the same methods used to make the ghast. You can make your own maze on cardstock or use one from a workbook. Use the smaller magnet on top of the maze and steer it with the larger magnet under the paper.

❄ Try pushing magnets around by placing their like poles together. You could even create a magnetic car and "drive" it with a larger magnet.

CAVE SPIDER CIRCUITS

Mix up a simple dough that provides the electrical pathway for illuminated eyes.

Abandoned mine shafts are lucky finds in Minecraft, but watch your back! Lurking in the tiniest of cracks are **CAVE SPIDERS**. Small, fast, and poisonous, cave spiders are among the deadliest mobs. Create your own version of these creepy critters with play dough that **CONDUCTS ELECTRICITY** and watch their eerie red eyes light up.

INSTRUCTIONS

Conductive Dough

1. Mix water, 1 cup of flour, salt, cream of tartar, vegetable oil, and food coloring together in a medium pan.

2. Have an adult help you cook the mixture over medium heat, stirring constantly. Remove from the heat when the mixture forms a ball that pulls away from the sides of the pan.

3. Allow the dough to cool.

4. Knead additional flour into the dough until it reaches desired consistency.

Insulating Dough

1. Mix 1 cup of flour with the sugar, oil, and food coloring (if using) in a bowl.

2. Add 1 tablespoon of deionized water. Stir until the water is absorbed.

3. Continue repeating Step 2 until large, sandy lumps begin to form.

4. Turn the dough out onto a floured surface, and gather into a single lump.

5. Add small amounts of flour and/or water until the dough reaches desired consistency.

Dough may be stored in a sealed container for several weeks or frozen for longer.

TIME

30 minutes to make dough

60 minutes to cool

30 minutes to make spider

MATERIALS

Conductive Dough

◆ 1 cup water

◆ 1 + ½ cups flour

◆ ¼ cup salt

◆ 3 tablespoons cream of tartar

◆ 1 tablespoon vegetable oil

◆ 20–30 drops black food coloring (available at craft stores)

Insulating Dough

(optional; modeling clay can be used instead)

◆ 1½ cups of flour (divided use)

◆ ½ cup sugar

◆ 3 tablespoons vegetable oil

◆ ½ cup deionized water

◆ 20–30 drops food coloring (if desired)

Spider

◆ 2 red LED 5-mm lightbulbs

◆ 1 9V battery

◆ battery holder for 9V battery (different combinations of batteries and a matching holder will also work)

Spider

1. Use the black conducting dough to make a spider. You will need to separate the conducting dough used on the head from the conducting dough used on the body/legs. (You can use the insulating dough between the head and the body to avoid a short circuit.)

2. Separate the terminals on the LED lights by gently pushing them apart into a V shape. (Notice that the terminals on the LED lights are different lengths. The longer terminal will need to be in the same piece of conducting dough as the red battery pack wire.)

3. Place the long terminal end of the LED lights in the head of the spider.

4. Place the short terminal end of the LED lights in the body of the spider.

5. Insert the black battery pack wire in the head.

6. Insert the red battery pack wire in the body.

7. The spider eyes should light up! If they don't light, double check that you have everything placed properly. Also, make sure the two pieces of conducting dough (the head and the body) are not touching each other.

WHAT REALLY HAPPENED?

❄ **ELECTRICITY** powers many of the things you use every day, such as your TV, lights, computer, and refrigerator. When you add electricity to conductive play dough, you can power lights, buzzers, and even motors by making a circuit.

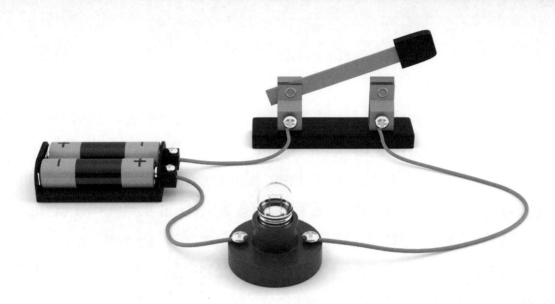

A **CIRCUIT** is a path through which electricity flows. It consists of a **CONDUCTOR** (something that allows electricity to flow, such as a wire) and an **INSULATOR** (something that does not allow electricity to flow, such as wood). The conductive play dough used salt and water as conductors. The insulating dough did not allow electricity to pass through.

Circuits need a source of electricity. In your home, you plug appliances into the wall. The electricity that comes to your home is from power plants. Smaller devices that require a power source use a battery, just like we used here.

YOUR TURN TO EXPERIMENT

What other creations can you make with the conducting dough? You can also use motors, buzzers, and more LED lights.

Test other types of clay or dough for their conductivity or resistance. You can even test materials such as wood, rubber, and fabric to find out if they are conductors or resistors.

ELYTRA WING GLIDER PERFORMANCE TEST

Compare the performance of Elytra wings to toy gliders, recording distance, time, and speed.

Perhaps you have soared through the End on Elytra wings. This cape-like tool allows Minecrafters to glide similar to the way a real-life hang-glider works. Since gliders do not have engines, players must jump to start gliding. How well does the **DESIGN OF THE ELYTRA WING** in Minecraft compare with the **DESIGN OF REAL-LIFE GLIDERS?** In this activity, you will make an Elytra wing glider and a toy glider similar to actual gliders. Then, you will collect measurements and data to compare their performance.

INSTRUCTIONS

Elytra Wing Glider

1. Use tracing paper to trace over the Elytra wing pattern on page 94.

2. Cut out the pattern and place on top of the foam plate. The wings may include the curved edge of the plate. Trace the pattern using a pen. (Hint: if it is difficult to trace around the tracing paper, glue it onto a piece of cardstock and then cut it out again. Now use the cardstock as a pattern.)

3. Cut out the foam, following the pattern.

4. Notice that there is a slit between the wings and on the tail. Cut along the slits and attach the tail by sliding the slots together. Use tape to secure the tail to the wings.

5. Attach a penny on top of the wings in front of the square tab where marked on the original pattern. Fold the tab back over the penny and use tape to keep it in place.

6. Gently toss the glider in front of you, then make any adjustments needed.

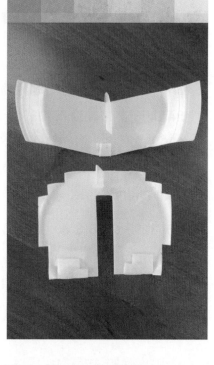

Toy Glider

1. Repeat Steps 1–4 using the toy glider pattern on page 95.

2. Attach a penny to the front of the toy glider in front of the square tab, where marked on the original pattern. Fold the tab back over the penny and use tape to keep it in place.

3. Gently toss the glider in front of you, then make any adjustments needed.

Performance Test

1. Stand at the top of your stairs or on a safe balcony or a play structure with your gliders.

2. Have a friend say go and start the stopwatch as you propel the Elytra glider into the air. The stopwatch should be stopped when the glider touches down on the ground. Record the time, in seconds, in the table on page 93.

3. Measure, in inches or centimeters, how far the Elytra glider traveled. Record the distance in the table.

4. Test your Elytra wing glider two more times, recording the time and distance each time.

TIME
30 minutes

MATERIALS

◆ tracing paper or thin, white printer paper

◆ 2 foam dinner plates (10.25 inches or 26 cm, no divided sections)

◆ pen

◆ scissors

◆ invisible tape

◆ 3 pennies

◆ tape measure

◆ stopwatch

◆ a friend

5. Next, test your toy glider using the same procedure described in Steps 1–4.

6. Calculate the average time and distance of each glider. Average can be calculated by adding the three times (or distances) together and then dividing by 3. Record the average in the table.

7. Calculate the speed of your gliders by dividing the distance by the time. For example, if your glider traveled 300 centimeters in 5 seconds, then the calculation would be:

$$300 \text{ centimeters (cm)} \div 5 \text{ seconds (s)} = 60 \text{ cm/s}$$

8. Record your results.

WHAT REALLY HAPPENED?

❋ **GLIDERS** are simply aircraft without engines. There are many different types of gliders, including paper airplanes and hang gliders. Did you know the space shuttle returns to Earth basically as a glider?

❋ Because gliders do not have engines, some other **FORCE** must be used to start their movement. In this activity, your hand was the force that propelled the glider. Hang gliders may run or jump off a hill to get going. Other gliders are towed by aircraft and then cut loose to begin their glide.

❋ In order to stay in the air, the wings on a glider must produce enough **LIFT** to balance the weight of the glider. Lift is the force that holds the glider in the air. To generate lift, a glider must move through the air.

YOUR TURN TO EXPERIMENT

✳ Experiment with other glider designs. Can you design a glider that stays in the air longer than the ones you made in this project?

✳ Challenge friends to a glider engineering contest. Compete to see whose glider stays in the air the longest time and whose glider travels the longest distance.

ELYTRA WING GLIDER RESULTS

	Distance	Time
Trial 1		
Trial 2		
Trial 3		
Average:		

TOY GLIDER RESULTS

	Distance	Time
Trial 1		
Trial 2		
Trial 3		
Average:		

AVERAGE SPEED OF ELYTRA WING GLIDER:

Average Distance = _____

Average Time = _____

Time ÷ Distance = _____

AVERAGE SPEED OF TOY GLIDER:

Average Distance = _____

Average Time = _____

Time ÷ Distance = _____

ELYTRA WING GLIDER PATTERN

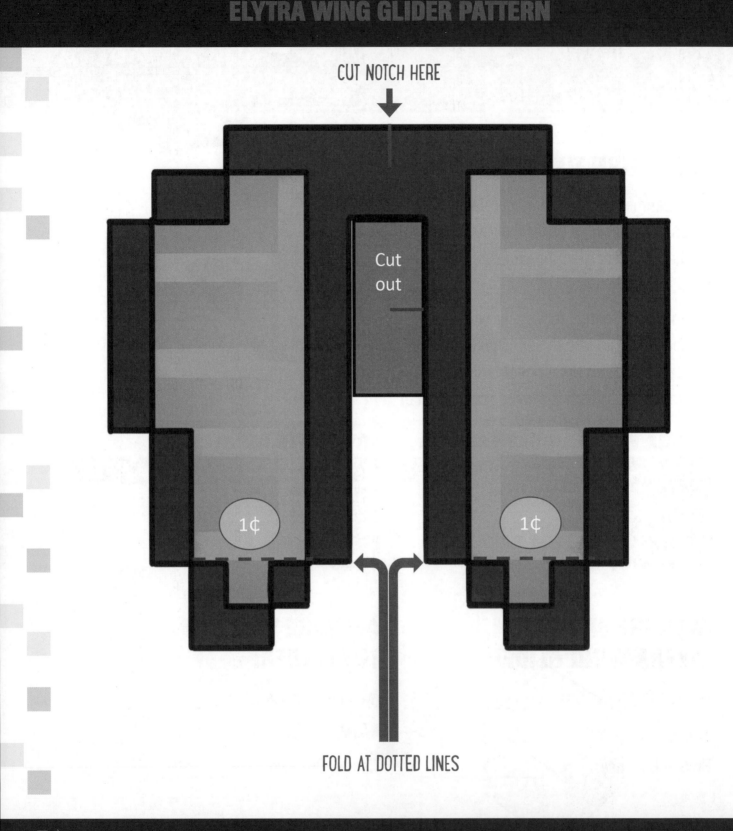

CUT NOTCH HERE

Cut out

1¢   1¢

FOLD AT DOTTED LINES

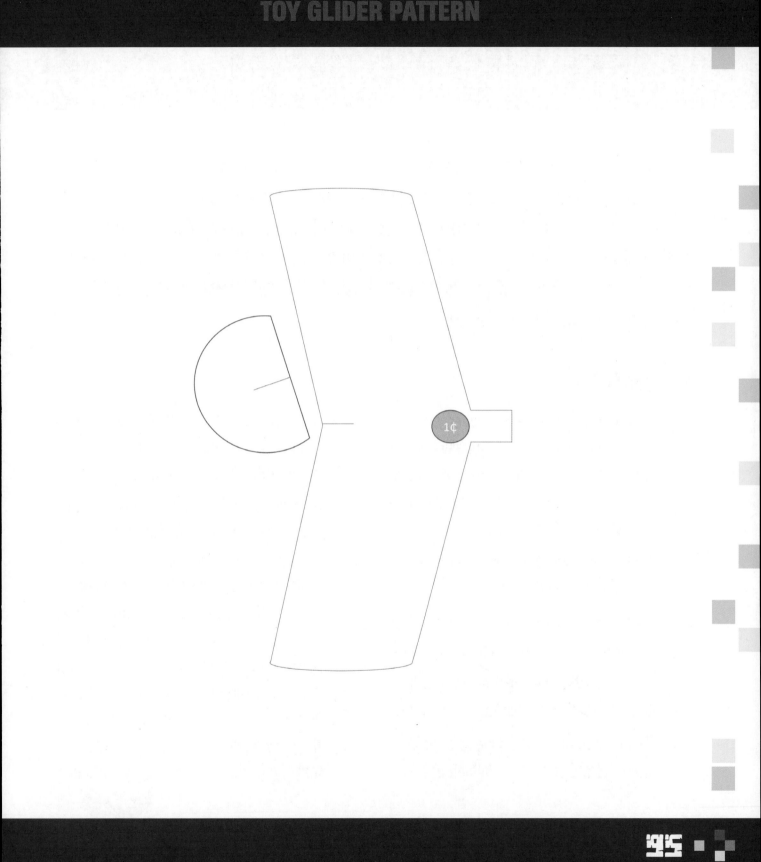

CRAFTING TABLE CHALLENGE

Build a sturdy table out of newspaper—all you need is a little engineering know-how.

A crafting table might be the first thing you learned to build in Minecraft. It only takes four planks, arranged in a square. Crafting tables allow players to craft blocks and make items from other materials. Can you build a table using only paper and tape? Even though paper is flimsy, it can be used to support heavy objects if you build with basic **ENGINEERING PRINCIPLES.** Ready to accept the challenge?

INSTRUCTIONS

1. Using one piece of newspaper, start at one corner and roll it diagonally toward the other corner. The first roll should be about the diameter of a straw. Use tape to keep the roll closed.

2. Make a second tube following the same procedure as in Step 1.

3. Bend one of the newspaper rolls into a square shape and use tape to secure it.

4. Bend the other newspaper roll into a triangle shape and use tape to secure it.

5. Push down on each shape and rock them from side to side. Which one is more stable? You will notice that the triangle will withstand more force and is more stable than the square.

6. Now, your challenge is to build a table using the remaining 8 sheets of newspaper and tape. Can you build a table that is 8 inches high (use your ruler) and strong enough to hold a book on a cardboard or foam board tabletop? Sketch your design on a piece of scrap paper and then get to work building! If your structure does not work the first time, try again. Brainstorm ways to make your table stronger. If your legs

MATERIALS

- 10 sheets of newspaper
- masking or packing tape
- ruler
- cardboard or foam board (8½ × 11 inches)
- book

twist under the weight of the book, how can you stabilize them? If your table wobbles, check to be certain it isn't lopsided. Did you use the strongest shape you can construct with newspaper?

WHAT REALLY HAPPENED?

❋ **TRIANGLES** are everywhere! Engineers use them all the time when designing structures that require strong and rigid construction. Squares are not as strong as triangles. When you pushed on the top of the square newspaper form, it leaned to the side and created a different structure called a rhombus.

❋ When you pushed down on the triangular newspaper form, it did not collapse the way the square did. Its strength came from the angles. The **ANGLES** helped the triangle maintain its shape.

YOUR TURN TO EXPERIMENT

❋ Try making a three-dimensional triangle and comparing its shape with the two-dimensional triangle you made earlier in the activity. You will need to make 6 newspaper tubes and connect them with tape (electrical tape works well for this activity). Compare its strength with the two-dimensional triangle.

MATH FOR MINECRAFTERS

UNDERSTANDING PLACE VALUE

I don't need my calculator for these problems!

Use place value to solve the problems.

1. 5,000 + 600 + 30 + 3 = _____

2. 2,000 + 60 + 1 = _____

3. 7,000 + 200 + 80 = _____

4. 3,000 + 400 + 90 + 1 = _____

5. 9,000 + 100 + 20 = _____

6. 8,000 + 500 + 70 + 6 = _____

7. 1,000 + 900 + 90 + 9 = _____

8. 4,000 + 3 = _____

NUMBERS TO 1,000

Write the number that goes between.

1. 4,893 [| | |] 4,895

2. 5,000 [| | |] 5,002

3. 3,999 [| | |] 4,001

4. 6,821 [| | |] 6,823

5. 1,739 [| | |] 1,741

6. 7,013 [| | |] 7,015

7. 9,001 [| | |] 9,003

8. 8,220 [| | |] 8,222

EXPLODING NUMBERS

Creeper has been exploding some numbers.
Use place value to write the missing numbers.

1. 2,496 = 2,000 + 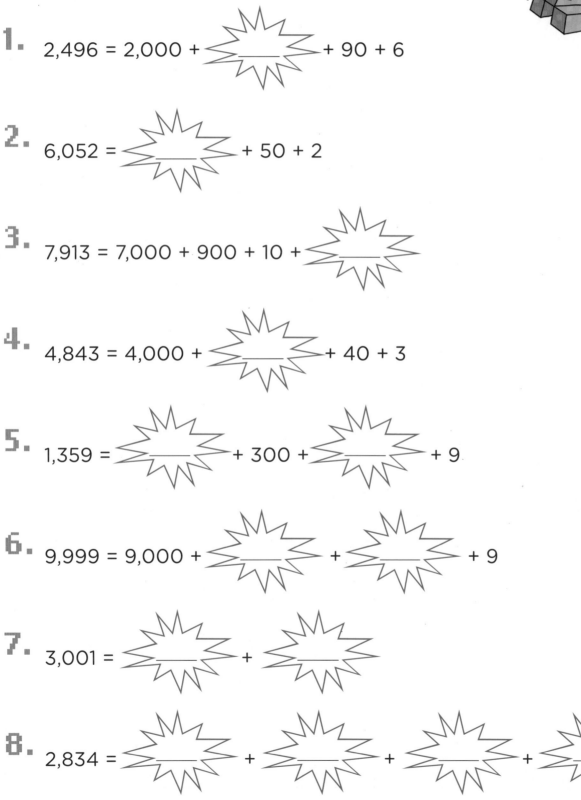 + 90 + 6

2. 6,052 = _____ + 50 + 2

3. 7,913 = 7,000 + 900 + 10 + _____

4. 4,843 = 4,000 + _____ + 40 + 3

5. 1,359 = _____ + 300 + _____ + 9

6. 9,999 = 9,000 + _____ + _____ + 9

7. 3,001 = _____ + _____

8. 2,834 = _____ + _____ + _____ + _____

ADD TO 100

Draw each problem using lines for tens and dots for ones. Then count and add. The first one is done for you.

$| = 10$ $\cdot = 1$

1.

33
+ 52
85

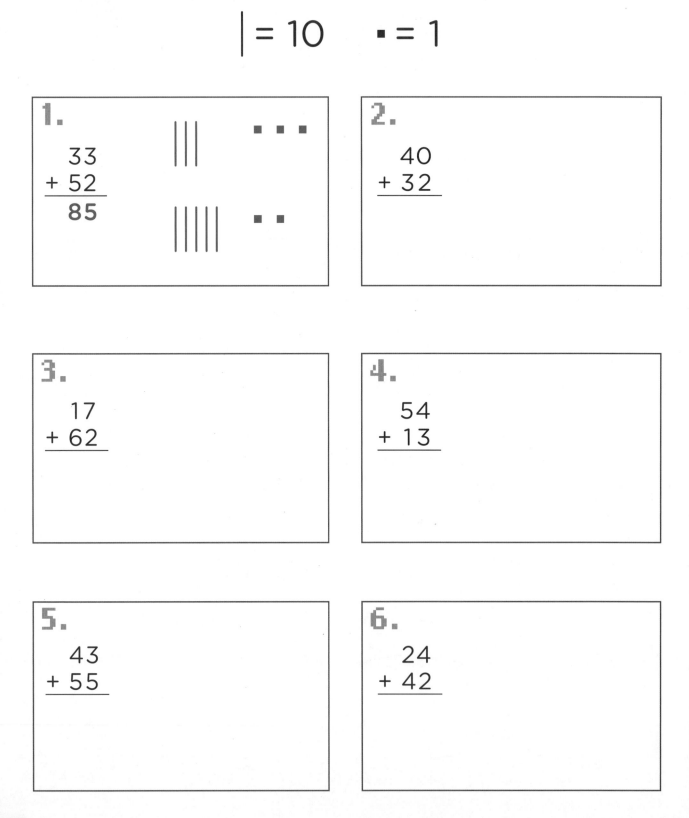

2.

40
+ 32

3.

17
+ 62

4.

54
+ 13

5.

43
+ 55

6.

24
+ 42

ADD TO 100

Solve each problem. Use the answers to solve the riddle.

1. 61 + 27	2. 55 + 32	3. 73 + 26	4. 42 + 23

O	T	R	F

5. 71 + 26	6. 12 + 51	7. 83 + 10	8. 73 + 25

B	M	S	C

9. 53 + 33	10. 38 + 51	11. 64 + 15	12. 36 + 41

V	H	I	E

Q: *Why does witch like to stay in a hotel?*

COPY THE LETTERS FROM THE ANSWERS ABOVE TO FIND OUT.

65   88   99   87   89   77   97   99   88   88   63

93   77   99   86   79   98   77

SUBTRACT WITHIN 100

| = 10   • = 1

Draw lines and dots to show the first number. Then cross out the second number. Count the amount that's left. The first one is done for you.

1.

57
− 16
41

2.

79
− 43

3.

28
− 13

4.

67
− 26

5.

86
− 72

6.

45
− 22

SUBTRACT WITHIN 100

Solve each problem. Use the answers to solve the riddle.

1. 77
− 23

2. 56
− 22

3. 49
− 17

4. 67
− 41

I

K

B

R

5. 99
− 46

6. 43
− 31

7. 65
− 35

8. 77
− 46

T

O

L

C

9. 98
− 34

10. 47
− 14

11. 59
− 14

12. 85
− 14

A

P

H

E

Q: *How do you stop hostile mobs from attacking you?*
COPY THE LETTERS FROM THE ANSWERS ABOVE TO FIND OUT.

___ ___ ___ ___ ___   ___ ___ ___ ___ ___
32   30   12   31   34   53   45   71   54   26

___ ___ ___ ___
33   64   53   45

ADDITION WITH REGROUPING

| = 10   • = 1

Draw lines and dots to show the numbers. Then combine the ones. Regroup to make ten. Then combine the tens. The first one is done for you.

1.

$$
\begin{array}{r}
{}^{1}34 \\
+\ 18 \\
\hline
52
\end{array}
$$

2.

$$
\begin{array}{r}
29 \\
+\ 43 \\
\end{array}
$$

3.

$$
\begin{array}{r}
28 \\
+\ 13 \\
\end{array}
$$

4.

$$
\begin{array}{r}
67 \\
+\ 28 \\
\end{array}
$$

5.

$$
\begin{array}{r}
56 \\
+\ 14 \\
\end{array}
$$

6.

$$
\begin{array}{r}
45 \\
+\ 37 \\
\end{array}
$$

ADDITION WITH REGROUPING

Solve the problems. Use the answers to solve the riddle.

1. $\begin{array}{r} 36 \\ + 24 \\ \hline \end{array}$ **2.** $\begin{array}{r} 49 \\ + 37 \\ \hline \end{array}$ **3.** $\begin{array}{r} 65 \\ + 18 \\ \hline \end{array}$ **4.** $\begin{array}{r} 52 \\ + 49 \\ \hline \end{array}$

A   K   B   T

5. $\begin{array}{r} 68 \\ + 27 \\ \hline \end{array}$ **6.** $\begin{array}{r} 39 \\ + 46 \\ \hline \end{array}$ **7.** $\begin{array}{r} 87 \\ + 18 \\ \hline \end{array}$ **8.** $\begin{array}{r} 71 \\ + 39 \\ \hline \end{array}$

U   I   E   H

9. $\begin{array}{r} 45 \\ + 26 \\ \hline \end{array}$ **10.** $\begin{array}{r} 17 \\ + 64 \\ \hline \end{array}$ **11.** $\begin{array}{r} 55 \\ + 29 \\ \hline \end{array}$ **12.** $\begin{array}{r} 25 \\ + 47 \\ \hline \end{array}$

S   C   N   L

Q: *Why is squid always giggling?*

COPY THE LETTERS FROM THE ANSWERS ABOVE TO FIND OUT.

| 83 | 105 | 81 | 60 | 95 | 71 | 105 | | 85 | 91 | 110 | 60 | 71 |

—

| 101 | 105 | 84 | | 101 | 85 | 81 | 86 | 72 | 105 | 71 |

SUBTRACTION WITH REGROUPING

| = 10   • = 1

Draw lines and dots to show the first number. Regroup a ten into ten ones. Then cross out the second number. Count the amount that's left. The first one is done for you.

1.

$\begin{array}{r} {}^{4}\cancel{5}{}^{1}2 \\ - \ 14 \\ \hline 38 \end{array}$

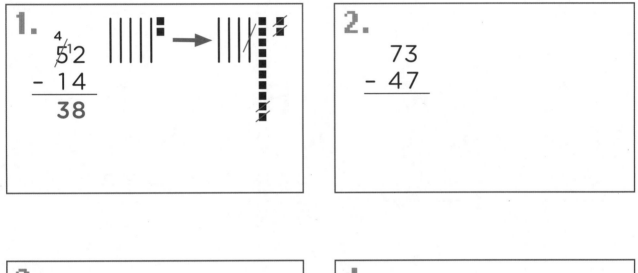

2.

$\begin{array}{r} 73 \\ - \ 47 \\ \hline \end{array}$

3.

$\begin{array}{r} 48 \\ - \ 19 \\ \hline \end{array}$

4.

$\begin{array}{r} 63 \\ - \ 28 \\ \hline \end{array}$

5.

$\begin{array}{r} 86 \\ - \ 38 \\ \hline \end{array}$

6.

$\begin{array}{r} 55 \\ - \ 27 \\ \hline \end{array}$

SUBTRACTION WITH REGROUPING

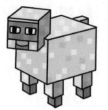

Solve the problems. Use the answers to solve the riddle.

1.
```
  83
- 29
────
```

2.
```
  76
- 38
────
```

3.
```
  41
- 27
────
```

A
4.
```
  80
- 45
────
```

P
5.
```
  74
- 26
────
```

B
6.
```
  52
- 37
────
```

T
7.
```
  91
- 54
────
```

O
8.
```
  70
- 24
────
```

E
9.
```
  55
- 29
────
```

S   P   H

Q: *Where does sheep go to be sheared?*

COPY THE LETTERS FROM THE ANSWERS ABOVE TO FIND OUT.

| 35 | 48 | | 35 | 26 | 15 | | 14 | 54 | 54 |

| 14 | 54 | 54 | | 37 | 26 | 48 | 46 |

MATH IN THE DESERT

Read and solve each problem. Use the box to show how you solved the problem.

1. The desert had 37 dead bushes and 15 cacti. How many plants were in the desert?

_____

2. One llama spawned 17 baby llamas. Another llama spawned 28 baby llamas. How many baby llamas were there?

_____

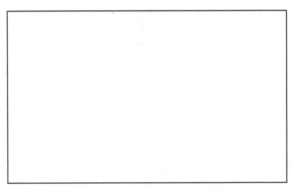

3. There were 52 baby llamas wandering in the desert, and 37 of them became adult llamas. How many baby llamas were left?

_____

4. Husk found two chests. The first chest was filled with 46 diamonds and the other was filled with 39 diamonds. How many more diamonds were in the first chest than in the second chest?

_____

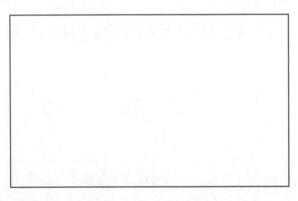

MATH IN THE MINES

Read and solve each problem. Use the box to show how you solved the problem.

1. Steve found 57 gems in the mine. He loaded 38 of the gems in the cart. How many gems were left in the mine?

_____

2. Steve found 75 emeralds and 27 diamonds. How many gems did he find in all?

_____

3. Alex found 46 diamonds and Steve found 27 diamonds. How many more diamonds did Alex find than Steve found?

_____

4. Alex found 46 diamonds and she found some emeralds too. She found 18 more diamonds than emeralds. How many emeralds did she find?

_____

MULTIPLYING MOBS

Yikes! These mobs are multiplying!

Read the problem. Draw a picture to solve.

1. Eight spiders were climbing up the wall. Each spider has 8 legs. How many spider legs are there in all?

_____ spider legs

2. Nine groups of zombie villagers were sitting in groups of 3. How many zombie villagers are there all together?

_____ zombie villagers

3. The skeletons were marching in a line. There were 7 rows of skeletons with 6 skeletons in each row. How many skeletons were marching?

_____ skeletons

4. Creepers were hiding behind the trees. There were 8 trees and 4 creepers behind each tree. How many creepers were hiding?

_____ creepers

MULTIPLICATION ARRAYS

Write multiplication equations to tell how many blocks are in each wall of redstone. The first one is done for you.

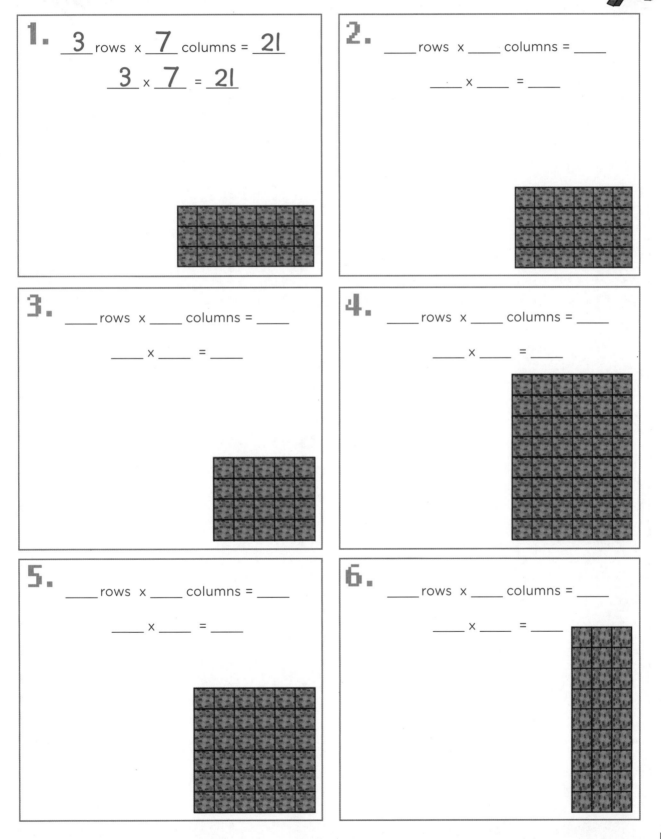

1. ___3___ rows x ___7___ columns = ___21___

___3___ x ___7___ = ___21___

2. _____ rows x _____ columns = _____

_____ x _____ = _____

3. _____ rows x _____ columns = _____

_____ x _____ = _____

4. _____ rows x _____ columns = _____

_____ x _____ = _____

5. _____ rows x _____ columns = _____

_____ x _____ = _____

6. _____ rows x _____ columns = _____

_____ x _____ = _____

MULTIPLICATION CHART

Complete the multiplication chart.

x	0	1	2	3	4	5	6	7	8	9	10
0	0										
1					4						
2											20
3				9							
4									32		
5						25					
6											
7		7									
8											
9				27							
10											100

MULTIPLICATION FACTS

Solve the problems. Use the key to color the orb.

Key:
- 8, 9, 10
- 12
- 14, 15, 16
- 18, 21, 25
- 4, 6, 20
- 5, 27, 28, 30, 32, 56
- 35, 36, 42, 49, 54, 64, 72, 81

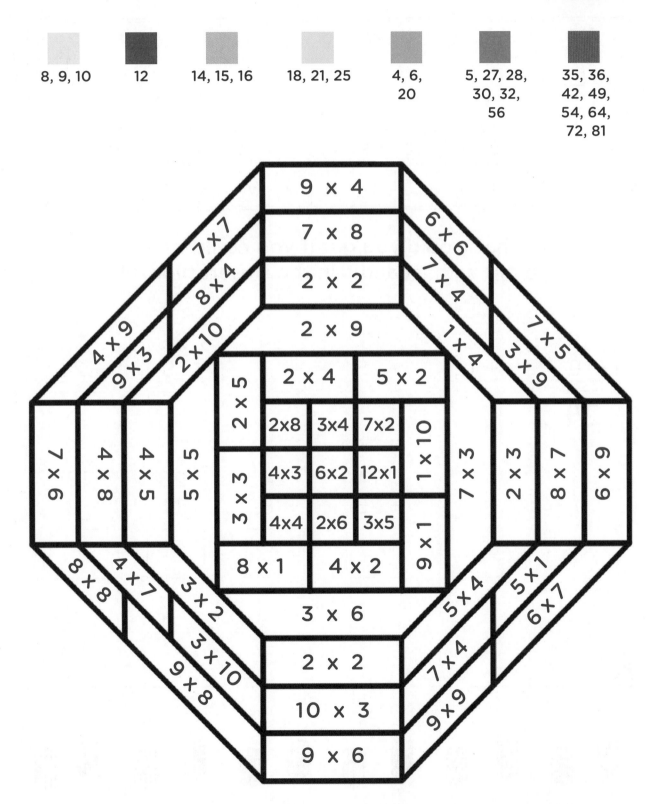

A PRICKLY SUBJECT

Find the sums of the math problems, then use the code-breaker key to reveal the answer to the joke.

24	25	26	27	28	29	30	31	32	33	34	35	36	37	38
A	B	C	D	E	F	G	H	I	J	K	L	M	N	O

39	40	41	42	43	44	45	46	47	48	49
P	Q	R	S	T	U	V	W	X	Y	Z

What would you get if you could breed a pig with a cactus in the Desert biome?

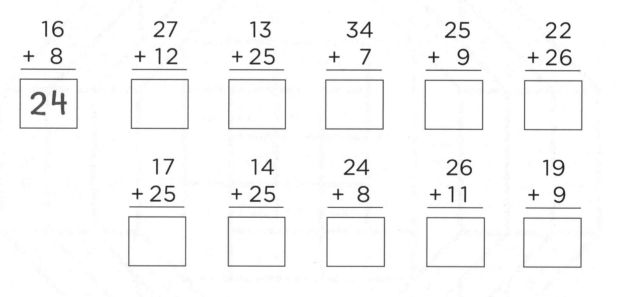

16 + 8	27 + 12	13 + 25	34 + 7	25 + 9	22 + 26
24					

17 + 25	14 + 25	24 + 8	26 + 11	19 + 9

A _ _ _ _ _ _ _ _ _ _ _

IN THE BALANCE

Time to rack up some experience!

The first scale is balanced. You must balance the second scale before it tips, lands on the pressure plate, and launches a hidden arrow right at you!

How many ⬡ do you need to balance the second scale? Draw them or write the number on the scale.

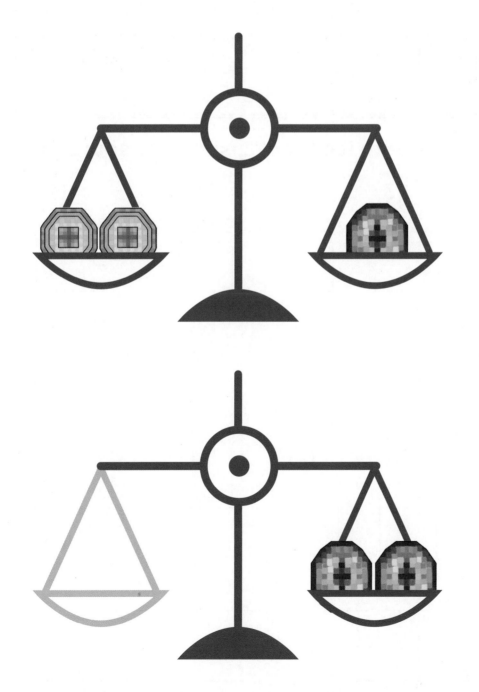

TREAT YOURSELF TO THIS TRICK

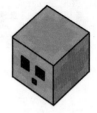

Solve the math problems, then use the code-breaker key to treat yourself to a trick you can play on your Minecrafting friends.

32	33	34	35	36	37	38	39	40	41	42	43	44	45	46
A	B	C	D	E	F	G	H	I	J	K	L	M	N	O

47	48	49	50	51	52	53	54	55	56	57
P	Q	R	S	T	U	V	W	X	Y	Z

Do this with ice blocks, slime, or soul sand:

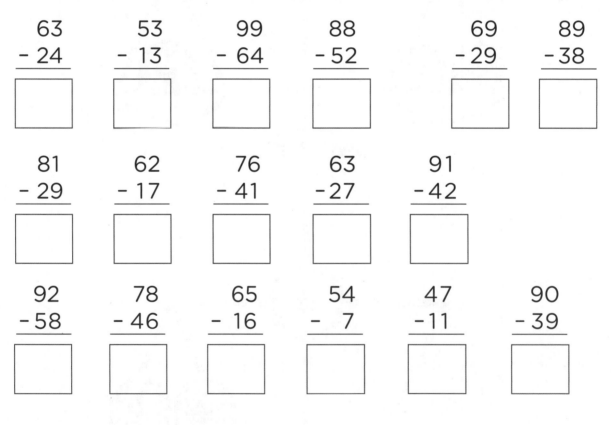

$$63 - 24 \qquad 53 - 13 \qquad 99 - 64 \qquad 88 - 52 \qquad 69 - 29 \qquad 89 - 38$$

$$81 - 29 \qquad 62 - 17 \qquad 76 - 41 \qquad 63 - 27 \qquad 91 - 42$$

$$92 - 58 \qquad 78 - 46 \qquad 65 - 16 \qquad 54 - 7 \qquad 47 - 11 \qquad 90 - 39$$

___ ___ ___ ___ ___ ___ ___

___ ___ ___ ___ ___ ___ ___ ___ ___ ___ ___

DON'T LET IT ROLL

The first scale is balanced. The second scale is not, and those spawn eggs are about to roll and start a dangerous chain reaction! How many  do you need to balance the second scale? Draw them or write the number on the scale.

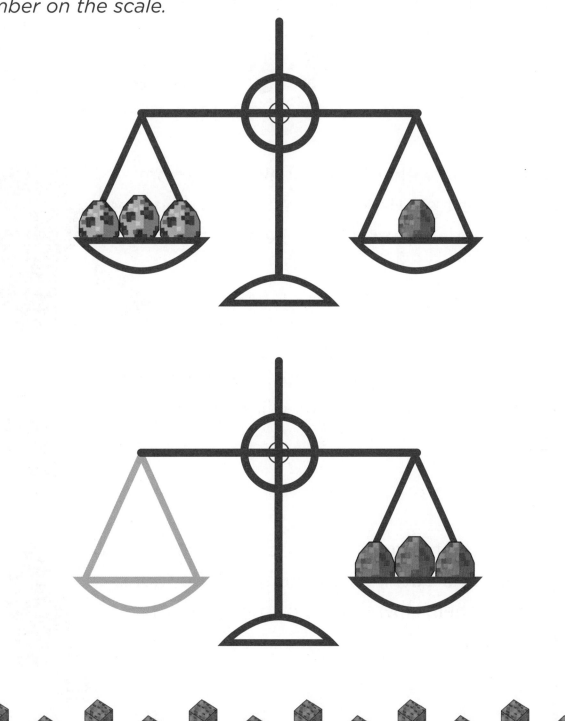

DIVISION

Solve the problems.

1. The chickens laid 20 eggs. There are 5 chickens. They each laid the same number of eggs. How many eggs did each chicken lay?

20 ÷ 5 = _____

2. Steve saw 12 wither heads peeking out from behind the tree. He knows that each wither has 3 heads. How many withers were in the tree?

12 ÷ 3 = _____

3. Steve needs 24 melon seeds. Each melon has 4 seeds. How many melons will Steve need?

24 ÷ 4 = _____

4. Witch had 21 potions. She had a case with 3 shelves. She put the same number of potions on each shelf. How many potions were on each shelf?

21 ÷ 3 = _____

DIGGING DIVISION

Read the problem and look at the picture.
Solve the problem.

1. Steve found 48 diamonds in the mine. He piled them into 6 piles. How many diamonds were in each pile?

48 ÷ 6 = _____

2. Steve had 27 emeralds and 3 chests. He put the same number of emeralds in each chest. How many emeralds were in each chest?

27 ÷ 3 = _____

3. Steve had 36 tin ingots. He stacked the ingots into 4 equal stacks. How many ingots were in each stack?

36 ÷ 4 = _____

4. Steve had 18 gold ingots. He stacked the gold ingots into 3 equal stacks. How many gold ingots were in each stack?

18 ÷ 3 = _____

FACT FAMILIES

Look at the fact families. Then fill in the missing numbers.

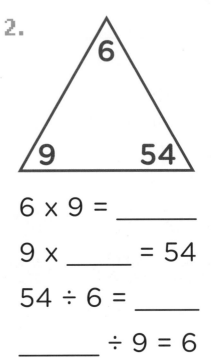

1.

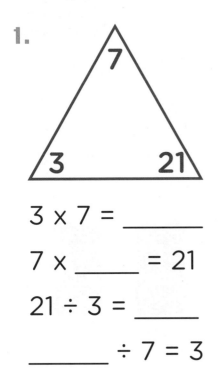

7

3   21

3 x 7 = _____

7 x _____ = 21

21 ÷ 3 = _____

_____ ÷ 7 = 3

2.

6

9   54

6 x 9 = _____

9 x _____ = 54

54 ÷ 6 = _____

_____ ÷ 9 = 6

3.

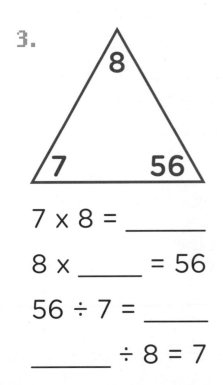

8

7   56

7 x 8 = _____

8 x _____ = 56

56 ÷ 7 = _____

_____ ÷ 8 = 7

4.

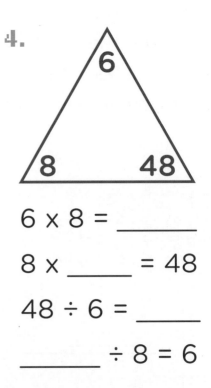

6

8   48

6 x 8 = _____

8 x _____ = 48

48 ÷ 6 = _____

_____ ÷ 8 = 6

DIVISION FACTS

Complete each equation.

1. $3 \times 4 =$ _____ $12 \div 3 =$ _____ $12 \div 4 =$ _____

2. $7 \times 6 =$ _____ $42 \div 6 =$ _____ $42 \div 7 =$ _____

3. $8 \times 5 =$ _____ $40 \div 8 =$ _____ $40 \div 5 =$ _____

4. $9 \times 4 =$ _____ $36 \div 9 =$ _____ $36 \div 4 =$ _____

5. $7 \times 5 =$ _____ $35 \div 7 =$ _____ $35 \div 5 =$ _____

6. $5 \times 9 =$ _____ $45 \div 5 =$ _____ $45 \div 9 =$ _____

7. $4 \times 6 =$ _____ $24 \div 4 =$ _____ $24 \div 6 =$ _____

8. $9 \times 7 =$ _____ $63 \div 9 =$ _____ $63 \div 7 =$ _____

MULTIPLYING BY TEN

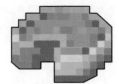

Multiply by ten. Find the pattern.

Multiplying by ten is as easy as pie!

1. 1 x 10 = _____

2. 2 x 10 = _____

3. 3 x 10 = _____

4. 4 x 10 = _____

5. 5 x 10 = _____

6. 6 x 10 = _____

7. 7 x 10 = _____

8. 8 x 10 = _____

9. 9 x 10 = _____

10. 10 x 10 = _____

11. 11 x 10 = _____

12. 12 x 10 = _____

What's the pattern?

_____

_____

MULTIPLYING BY TENS

Multiply by tens to solve the problems.

This isn't magic. It's math!

Hint: 3 x 4 = 12   3 x 40 = 120

1. 2 x 50 = _____

2. 6 x 40 = _____

3. 30 x 7 = _____

4. 60 x 6 = _____

5. 70 x 2 = _____

6. 4 x 80 = _____

7. 5 x 40 = _____

8. 3 x 90 = _____

9. 60 x 5 = _____

10. 4 x 70 = _____

11. 20 x 4 = _____

12. 50 x 6 = _____

13. 4 x 40 = _____

14. 3 x 50 = _____

15. 7 x 50 = _____

16. 20 x 6 = _____

MULTIPLYING WITHIN 100

This is like three problems in one!

Solve the problems. The first two are done for you.

43	Multiply the ones.	Multiply the tens.	Add.
x 2	$3 \times 2 = 6$	$40 \times 2 = 80$	$80 + 6 = 86$
86			

1.
```
  24
 x 2
   8
+40
  48
```

2.
```
  46
 x 2
  12
+80
  92
```

3.
```
 63
x 3
```

4.
```
 51
x 4
```

5.
```
 36
x 5
```

6.
```
 27
x 6
```

7.
```
 54
x 4
```

8.
```
 64
x 6
```

9.
```
 25
x 5
```

10.
```
 31
x 7
```

11.
```
 82
x 7
```

12.
```
 74
x 3
```

MULTIPLYING WITHIN 100

Solve the problems. Use the answer to solve the riddle.

1. 54
x 6

2. 26
x 5

3. 42
x 7

4. 73
x 5

5. 61
x 8

   U   H   R   A   S

6. 38
x 6

7. 24
x 3

8. 45
x 2

9. 56
x 4

10. 62
x 5

   O   C   D   T   N

11. 93
x 7

12. 44
x 5

13. 37
x 3

14. 43
x 7

   L   E   K   B

Q: *How does Steve stay in shape?*

COPY THE LETTERS FROM THE ANSWERS ABOVE TO FIND OUT.

130 220   294 324 310 488   365 294 228 324 310   90

224 130 220   301 651 228 72 111

DIVIDING BY TENS

Complete each equation.

1. $36 \div 9 = 4$

   $360 \div 9 = $ _____

   $360 \div 90 = $ _____

2. $64 \div 8 = 8$

   $640 \div 8 = $ _____

   $640 \div 80 = $ _____

3. $27 \div 9 = 3$

   $270 \div 9 = $ _____

   $270 \div 30 = $ _____

4. $42 \div 7 = 6$

   $420 \div 7 = $ _____

   $420 \div 70 = $ _____

5. $54 \div 9 = 6$

   $540 \div 9 = $ _____

   $540 \div 90 = $ _____

6. $49 \div 7 = 7$

   $490 \div 7 = $ _____

   $490 \div 70 = $ _____

7. $45 \div 5 = 9$

   $450 \div 5 = $ _____

   $450 \div 50 = $ _____

8. $56 \div 8 = 7$

   $560 \div 8 = $ _____

   $560 \div 80 = $ _____

9. $32 \div 4 = 8$

   $320 \div 4 = $ _____

   $320 \div 40 = $ _____

DIVISION

Solve the division problems. The first one is done for you.

1.
$$9\overline{)54} = 6$$

2.
$$8\overline{)72}$$

3.
$$6\overline{)36}$$

4.
$$8\overline{)32}$$

5.
$$4\overline{)24}$$

6.
$$2\overline{)18}$$

7.
$$7\overline{)21}$$

8.
$$5\overline{)35}$$

9.
$$8\overline{)64}$$

10.
$$9\overline{)63}$$

11.
$$6\overline{)54}$$

12.
$$9\overline{)27}$$

DIVIDING WITH REMAINDERS

Solve the division problems.

$$5\overline{)27} \quad \begin{array}{r} 5\ R2 \\ \hline 27 \\ -25 \\ \hline 2 \end{array}$$

Show what's left over using R.

1.

$$7\overline{)58}$$

2.

$$6\overline{)42}$$

3.

$$9\overline{)75}$$

4.

$$4\overline{)26}$$

5.

$$4\overline{)37}$$

6.

$$9\overline{)85}$$

7.

$$8\overline{)61}$$

8.

$$7\overline{)43}$$

9.

$$8\overline{)68}$$

10.

$$6\overline{)22}$$

11.

$$8\overline{)27}$$

12.

$$8\overline{)55}$$

DIVIDING WITHIN 100

Solve the division problems. Then use the answers to solve the riddle.

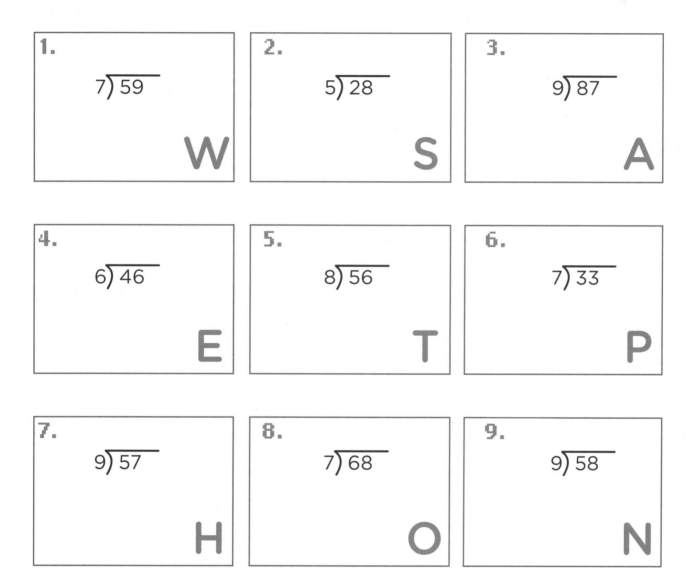

1.

7) 59

W

2.

5) 28

S

3.

9) 87

A

4.

6) 46

E

5.

8) 56

T

6.

7) 33

P

7.

9) 57

H

8.

7) 68

O

9.

9) 58

N

Q: *Where can you sell Minecraft eggs?*
COPY THE LETTERS FROM THE ANSWERS ABOVE TO FIND OUT.

$\overline{\text{9 R6}}$ $\quad$ $\overline{\text{9}}$ $\qquad$ $\overline{\text{7}}$ $\overline{\text{6 R3}}$ $\overline{\text{7 R4}}$ $\qquad$ $\overline{\text{5 R3}}$ $\overline{\text{4 R5}}$ $\overline{\text{9 R6}}$ $\overline{\text{8 R3}}$ $\overline{\text{6 R4}}$

$\overline{\text{5 R3}}$ $\overline{\text{6 R3}}$ $\overline{\text{9 R5}}$ $\overline{\text{4 R5}}$ •

MULTIPLES

A multiple is the product of a number when multipled by other numbers. **For example:** The multiples of 3 are

3,   6,   9,   12,   15,   and so on.

(3x1) (3x2) (3x3) (3x4) (3x5)

Fill in the missing multiples. Look for patterns of odd and even numbers.

1. Multiples of 2: 2, 4, 6, 8, ____ , 12, ____ , 16, 18, 20, ____ , ____ , 26

2. Multiples of 4: 4, ____ , ____ , 16, 20, ____ , ____ , 32, 36, ____ , ____

3. Multiples of 6: 6, 12, ____ , 24, 30, ____ , ____ , 48, ____ , ____ , 66

4. Multiples of 8: ____ , 16, 24, ____ , ____ , ____ , 56, ____ , 72, 80, ____

Multiples of even numbers are _____.

even / odd

5. Multiples of 5: 5, 10, ____ , 20, 25, ____ , ____ , 40, ____ , ____ , 55

6. Multiples of 7: 7, 14, ____ , 28, 35, ____ , 49, _____ , 63, _____ , 77

7. Multiples of 9: ____ , 18, 27, ____ , 45, ____ , _____ , 72, ____ , 90, ____

Multiples of odd numbers are _____ .

COMMON MULTIPLES

Common multiple are multiples that are the same for two numbers. **For example:** 4 and 8 are common multiples of 2 and 4.

2: 2, 4, 6, 8, 10

4: 4, 8, 12, 16

Use the lists of multiples you completed on the previous page to answer the questions.

1. Is 10 a common multiple of 2 and 4? Explain.

_____

2. What are the common multiples of 2 and 6?

_____

3. What number is a common multiple of 2, 4, and 6?

_____

4. What are the common multiples of 2 and 5?

_____

5. What are the common multiples of 6 and 9?

_____

6. What is the common multiple of 7 and 8?

_____

INSIDE RIDDLE

The letters in the code-breaker key spell the answers to both riddles below. Solve the math problems to decipher the answer to the first riddle. Then cross off those letters inside the code-breaker key to reveal the answer to the second riddle.

What large object sometimes generates on a beach?

13	14	15	16	17	18	19	20	21	22	23	24	25	26	27	28
I	S	H	C	I	E	P	W	B	R	E	E	R	C	K	G

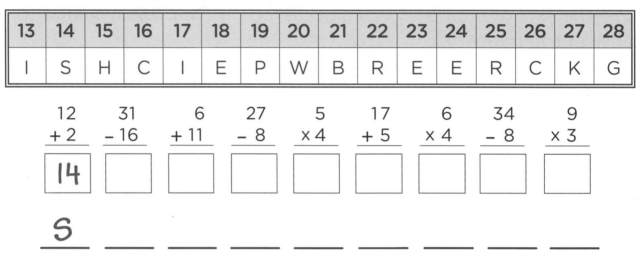

$$12 + 2 \qquad 31 - 16 \qquad 6 + 11 \qquad 27 - 8 \qquad 5 \times 4 \qquad 17 + 5 \qquad 6 \times 4 \qquad 34 - 8 \qquad 9 \times 3$$

| 14 | | | | | | | | |

S __ __ __ __ __ __ __ __

Where else does it generate?

__ __ __ __ __ __ __ __ __

134

UNDER PRESSURE

The first and second scales are balanced. How many ![die] do you need to balance the third scale? Draw them or write the number on the scale.

If you balance the scale correctly, you'll keep the blocks from rolling off the scale and avoid a dangerous chain reaction.

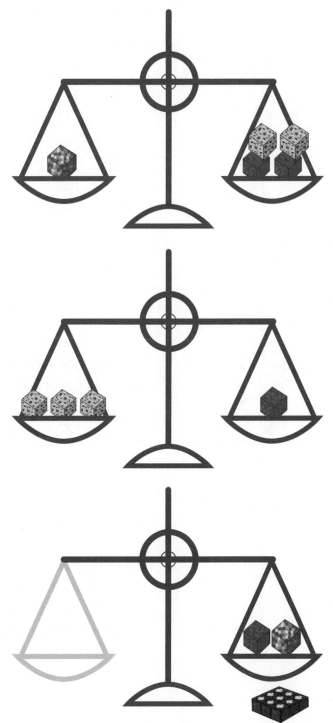

JUMP FIVE

Beginning with the number 19, jump from box to box by adding 5 each time you move. Write the letter from each box where you land on the blank letter spaces, in order from left to right. You'll reveal a Minecraft game where players jump around.

29 **R** 49	59 **N** 28	39 **O** 79
44 **U** 35	40 **E** 64	45 **A** 24
29 **P** (19)	9 **K** 34	8 **L** 22

Þ _ _ _ _ _ _ _

MAGIC NUMBER 1

The numbers at the end of the rows are linked to the images in the grid. What number goes in the circle? This is the magic number.

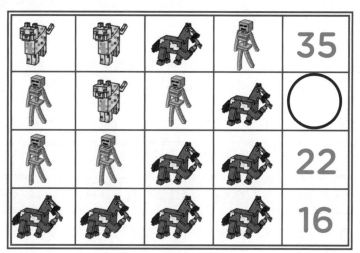

Circle the problems below that have the magic number as their answer. Unscramble those letters to spell the name of a Minecraft mob.

28 + 2	6 x5	26 + 4	33 – 22	17 +24	15 x 2
N	L	G	I	R	E

21 +9	51 –11	16 +14	76 –46	53 –23	42 –12
W	C	O	M	S	O

___ ___ ___ ___ ___ ___ ___ ___

ALERT! ALERT! ALERT!

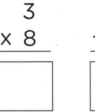

Use this handy trick to stay safe when you're working in your Minecraft house...or office...or lab...or anywhere indoors.

Solve the math problems, then use the code-breaker key to reveal this useful tip.

14	15	16	17	18	19	20	21	22	23	24	25	26	27	28
A	B	C	D	E	F	G	H	I	J	K	L	M	N	O

29	30	31	32	33	34	35	36	37	38	39
P	Q	R	S	T	U	V	W	X	Y	Z

If you want to hear when hostile mobs are approaching, surround your building with

18 + 11	5 × 5	22 − 8	54 ÷ 2	3 × 8	28 + 4
29					

Þ __ __ __ __ __ .

A BALANCED DIET

You've gotta eat to survive!

The first and second scales are balanced. How many  *do you need to balance the third scale? Draw them or write the number on the scale.*

If you balance the scale correctly, you will refill your hunger bar.

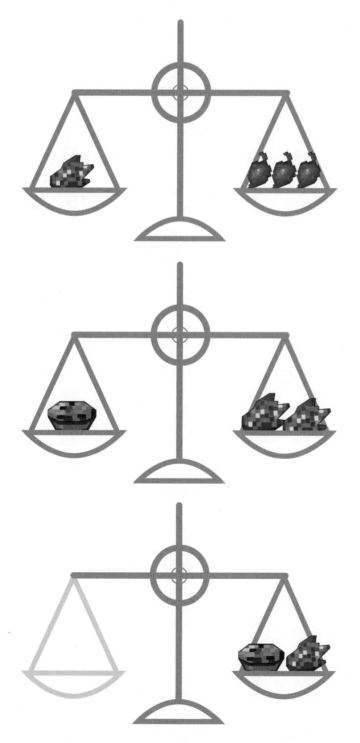

TWINZIES

Beginning with the number 75, count up by fives. Write the letter from each box where you land on the spaces, in order from left to right until all spaces are filled.

If you count, hop, and copy letters correctly, you'll reveal the answer to this question:

What do you call Alex's zombie twin?

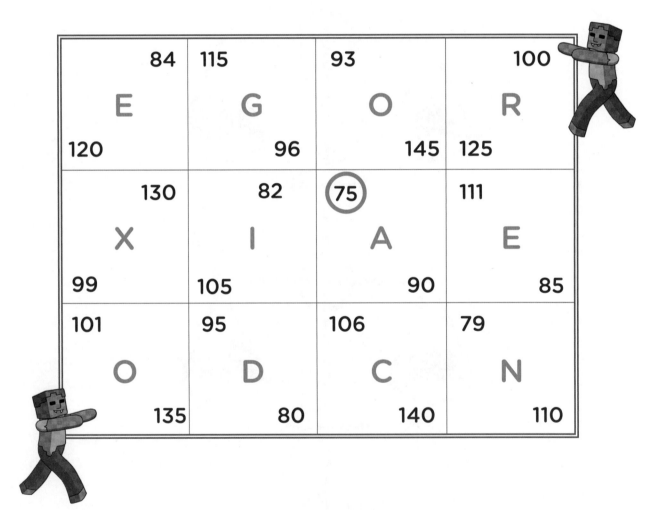

84 **E** 120	115 **G** 96	93 **O** 145	100 **R** 125
130 **X** 99	82 **I** 105	75 **A** 90	111 **E** 85
101 **O** 135	95 **D** 80	106 **C** 140	79 **N** 110

<u>A</u> __ __ __ __

__ __ __ __ __ __

MAGIC NUMBER 2

The numbers at the end of the rows are linked to the images in the grid. What number goes in the circle? This is the magic number for this puzzle.

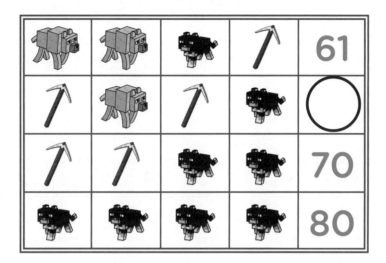

Circle the problems below that have the magic number as their answer. Unscramble those letters to reveal a play mode that gives you more control over the Minecraft world.

76 −13	8 ×7	45 + 2	7 ×9	91 −28
F	N	A	U	F

98 −34	47 +16	84 −19	21 × 3	28 +35
G	B	B	E	T

__ __ __ __ __ __ __

WHAT IS THE MEANING OF THIS?

Solve the math problems, then use the code-breaker key to reveal a fun fact about the company that makes Minecraft.

48	49	50	51	52	53	54	55	56	57	58	59	60	61	62
A	B	C	D	E	F	G	H	I	J	K	L	M	N	O

63	64	65	66	67	68	69	70	71	72	73
P	Q	R	S	T	U	V	W	X	Y	Z

$$20 \times 3 \quad 38 + 24 \quad 19 \times 3 \quad 96 \div 2 \quad 98 - 37 \quad 18 \times 3$$

" **60** ☐ ☐ ☐ ☐ ☐ " is a

M __ __ __ __ __

$$99 - 33 \quad 35 \times 2 \quad 43 + 9 \quad 17 \times 3 \quad 72 - 16 \quad 38 + 28 \quad 11 \times 5 \qquad 10 \times 7 \quad 18 + 44 \quad 84 - 19 \quad 93 - 42$$

☐ ☐ ☐ ☐ ☐ ☐ ☐   ☐ ☐ ☐ ☐

___ ___ ___ ___ ___ ___ ___ ___ ___ ___ ___

$$9 \times 6 \quad 29 + 19 \quad 73 - 22 \quad 48 + 6 \quad 71 - 19 \quad 33 + 34$$

meaning " ☐ ☐ ☐ ☐ ☐ ☐ . "

___ ___ ___ ___ ___ ___

PAYMENT BALANCE

Villagers insist you balance the payment scales below. If you don't, they vow to pillage your inventory.

The first and second scales are balanced. How many 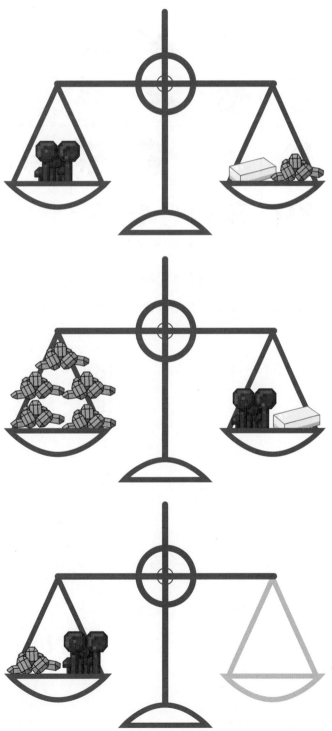 do you need to balance the third scale? Draw them or write the number on the scale.

MAGIC NUMBER 3

The numbers at the end of the rows and columns are linked to the images in the grid. What number goes in the circle? This is the magic number for this puzzle.

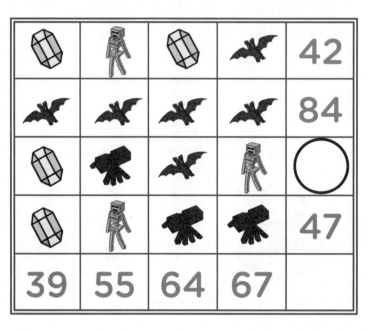

Circle the problems below that have the magic number as their answer. Unscramble those letters to reveal a clever way to locate hidden caves.

79 −25	13 ×4	64 −12	18 × 3	8 × 6	25 +27
E	O	S	A	D	P

78 −26	41 + 2	13 +39	26 × 2	80 +24
I	B	T	N	C

_ _ _ _ _ _

PRO BUILDER TIP

Design and build cool structures and scenes with this pro tip.

Use the picture-number combination under each blank letter space to find the correct letter on the grid. The correct letter is the one where the picture and number intersect. If you fill in the spaces correctly, you'll discover a unique method for crafting amazing buildings and landscapes.

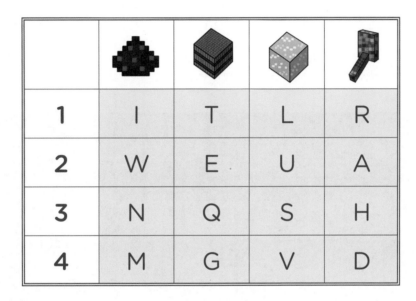

1	I	T	L	R
2	W	E	U	A
3	N	Q	S	H
4	M	G	V	D

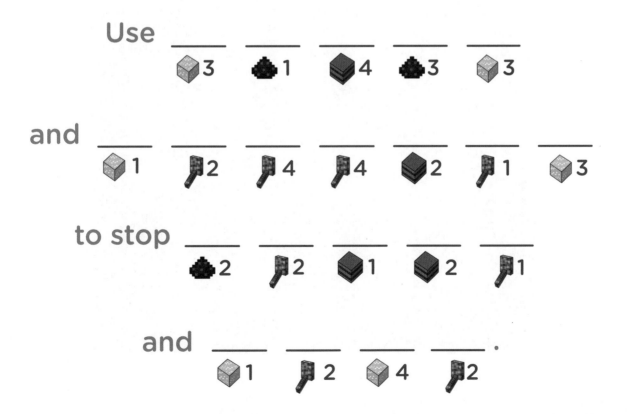

Use ____ ____ ____ ____ ____

and ____ ____ ____ ____ ____ ____ ____

to stop ____ ____ ____ ____ ____

and ____ ____ ____ ____ .

145

HIDDEN RESOURCE

Color the boxes that contain a multiple of 3.

33	15	81	86	75	39	24	70	66	30	72	11	72	3	18	34	75	19	87
8	90	76	35	42	89	51	43	93	91	87	82	36	55	96	74	99	61	57
26	48	41	20	96	14	78	1	6	12	54	2	21	59	79	25	15	60	24
77	63	67	47	36	83	45	88	54	81	32	65	9	17	42	68	51	80	39
49	9	22	40	21	69	18	71	84	94	90	85	48	66	84	46	78	13	45

NEIGHM YOUR HORSE

Is there such a thing as too many Minecraft jokes? Neigh!

Find the sums of the math problems, then use the code-breaker key to decipher the punchline of this joke.

48	49	50	51	52	53	54	55	56	57	58	59	60	61	62
A	B	C	D	E	F	G	H	I	J	K	L	M	N	O

63	64	65	66	67	68	69	70	71	72	73
P	Q	R	S	T	U	V	W	X	Y	Z

Alex calls her horse "Mayo," and

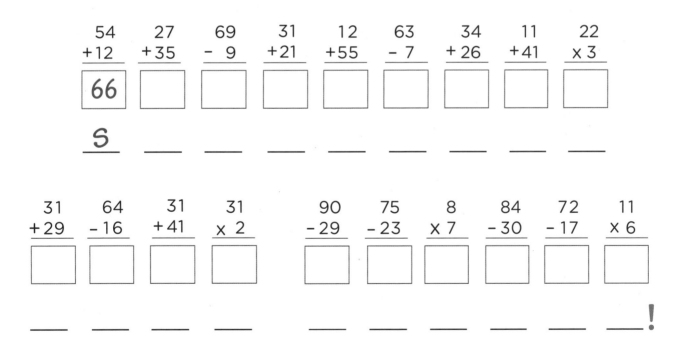

54 +12	27 +35	69 − 9	31 +21	12 +55	63 − 7	34 + 26	11 +41	22 x 3
66								
S	__	__	__	__	__	__	__	__

31 +29	64 −16	31 +41	31 x 2	90 − 29	75 − 23	8 x 7	84 − 30	72 − 17	11 x 6

__ __ __ __ __ __ __ __ __ __!

MAGIC NUMBER 4

The numbers at the end of the rows and columns are linked to the images in the grid. What number goes in the circle? This is the magic number for this puzzle.

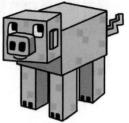

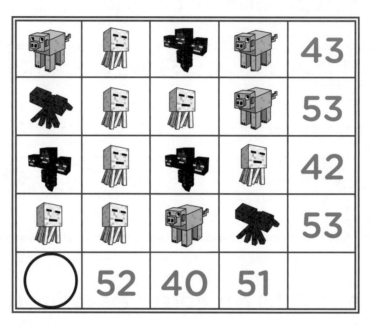

Circle the problems below that have the magic number as their answer. Unscramble those letters to spell the name of a Minecraft mob.

6	17	2	57	7	36
x 8	+31	x 24	- 9	x 7	+13

   S   I   H   L   A   B

60	12	33	4	16	29
-12	x 4	+15	x 12	x 3	+19

   R   S   V   F   E   I

_____ _____ _____ _____ _____ _____ _____ _____ _____

ZOMBIE-PROOF

Use the picture-number combination under each space to find the correct letter on the grid. The correct letter is the one where the picture and number intersect. If you fill in the spaces correctly, you'll discover a useful Minecraft tip for protecting yourself from zombies.

1	O	V	C	I
2	B	S	L	D
3	F	G	R	M
4	J	N	A	E

Want to zombie-proof your castle?

__ __ __ __ __ __
3   4   4   1   4   2

make excellent

__ __ __ __ __
2   1   1   3   2

149

MAGIC NUMBER 5

The numbers at the end of the rows and columns are linked to the images in the grid. What number goes in the circle? This is the magic number for this puzzle.

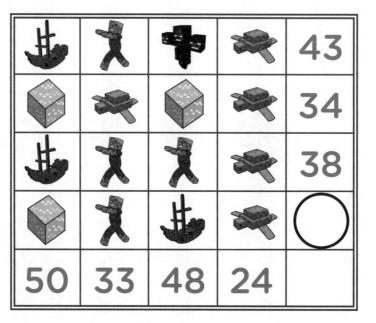

Circle the problems below that have the magic number as their answer. Unscramble those letters to spell the name of a new, underwater block that can be activated to attack hostile mobs.

8 x 5	18 +13	26 +14	48 - 8	4 x 10
D	E	I	U	C

57 -17	2 x20	47 - 9	62 x 2	27 +13
N	T	L	S	O

___ ___ ___ ___ ___ ___ ___

AIM HIGH

Reaching higher altitudes is possible only if you know this trick. Use the picture-number combination under each blank letter space to find the correct letter on the grid. The correct letter is the one where the picture and number intersect. If you fill in the spaces correctly, you'll discover a useful Minecraft skill.

	🦜	🛤	➶	🐉
1	L	N	E	J
2	C	U	P	G
3	I	S	T	R
4	O	A	M	K

___ ___ ___ ___ ___ ___
➶2 🦜3 🦜1 🦜1 🛤4 🐉3

___ ___ ___ ___ ___ ___ ___
🐉1 🛤2 ➶4 ➶2 🦜3 🛤1 🐉2

FALL FIX

Have you ever been destroyed in the game by a bad fall? Next time, use this to survive. Solve the math problems, then use the code-breaker key to reveal a handy tip for avoiding falls.

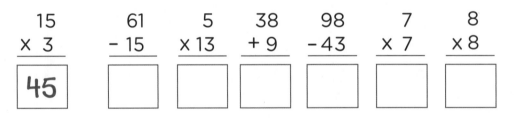

45	46	47	48	49	50	51	52	53	54	55	56	57	58	59
A	B	C	D	E	F	G	H	I	J	K	L	M	N	O

60	61	62	63	64	65	66	67	68	69	70
P	Q	R	S	T	U	V	W	X	Y	Z

$$\begin{array}{ccccccc}
15 & 61 & 5 & 38 & 98 & 7 & 8 \\
\times\ 3 & -\ 15 & \times\ 13 & +\ 9 & -\ 43 & \times\ 7 & \times\ 8 \\
\end{array}$$

45

A __ __ __ __ __ __

$$\begin{array}{ccccccc}
32 & 10 & 91 & 43 & 16 & 82 & 27 \\
+27 & \times\ 5 & -24 & +\ 2 & \times\ 4 & -33 & +35 \\
\end{array}$$

__ __ __ __ __ __ __

BALANCE OF NATURE

Can you preserve the delicate balance of nature? The first and second scales are balanced. How many 🌷 do you need to balance the third scale? Draw them or write the number on the scale.

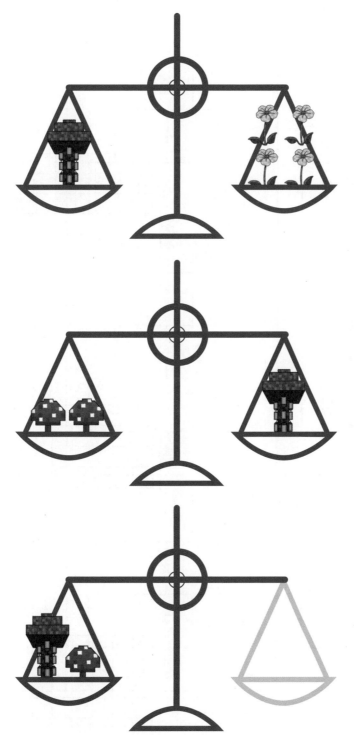

TREE MATH

Complete each tree. Each number is the answer to the two numbers below. Watch the signs **+**, **-**, **X**, **÷** . The first one is done for you.

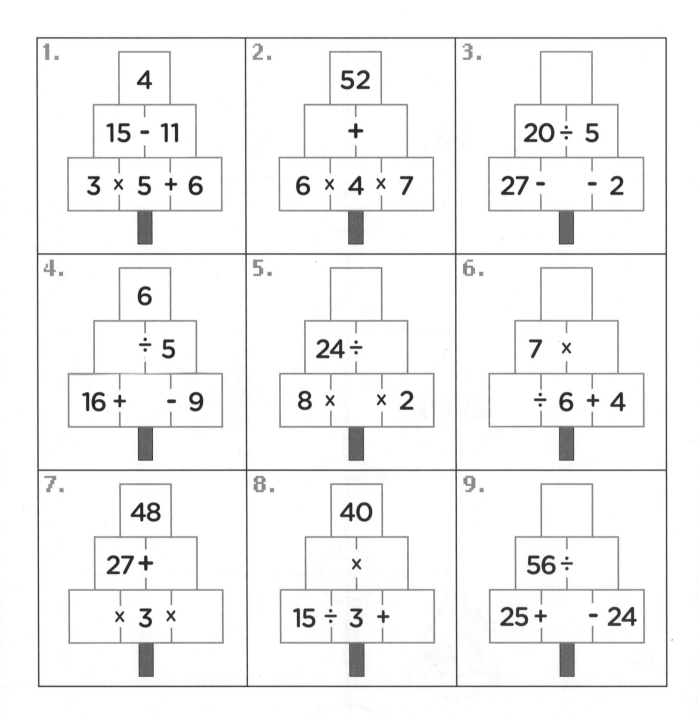

1.

4

15 - 11

3 × 5 + 6

2.

52

\+

6 × 4 × 7

3.

20 ÷ 5

27 -   - 2

4.

6

÷ 5

16 +   - 9

5.

24 ÷

8 ×   × 2

6.

7   ×

÷ 6 + 4

7.

48

27 +

× 3 ×

8.

40

×

15 ÷ 3 +

9.

56 ÷

25 +   - 24

BLOCK LOGIC

Use logic to determine the value of each block and solve the problems.

DIAMOND   BUSH   PRISMARINE   ICE   COBBLESTONE   CLAY

_____   _____   _____   _____   _____   _____

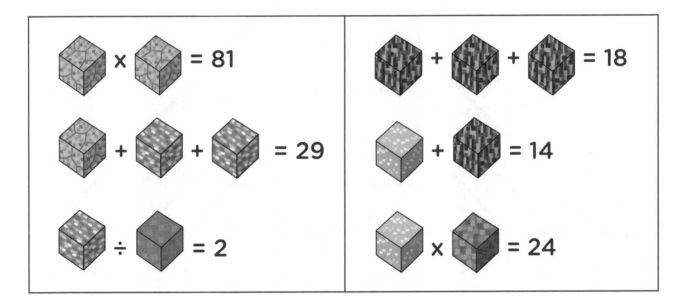

Solve the problems.

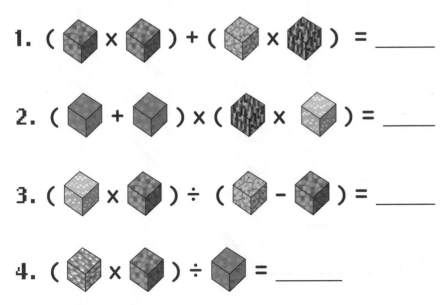

1. (▨ × ▨) + (▨ × ▨) = _____

2. (▨ + ▨) × (▨ × ▨) = _____

3. (▨ × ▨) ÷ (▨ − ▨) = _____

4. (▨ × ▨) ÷ ▨ = _____

FRACTION BARS

Label each fraction part. The first one is done for you.

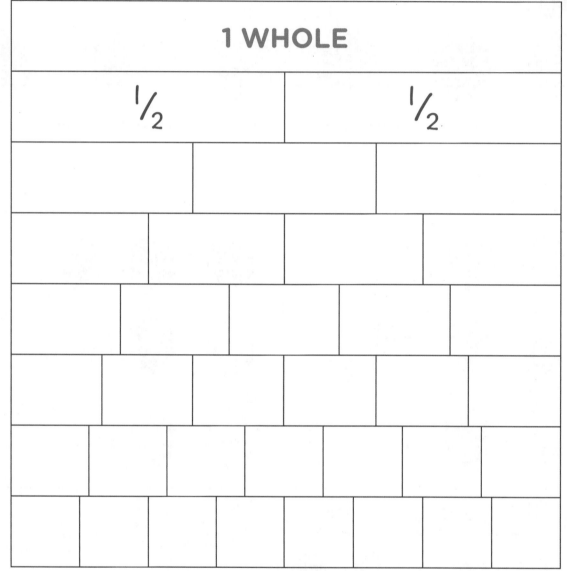

1 WHOLE

| ¹/₂ | ¹/₂ |

Use >, <, and = to compare the fractions.

1. ¹/₂ ☐ ¹/₃

2. ²/₄ ☐ ¹/₂

3. ³/₄ ☐ ⁵/₆

4. ¹/₅ ☐ ⁴/₈

5. ²/₃ ☐ ⁴/₆

6. ¹/₃ ☐ ³/₅

HUNGER FRACTIONS

Read the hunger bars. Use fractions to answer the questions.

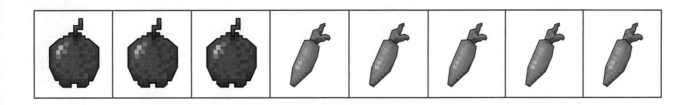

1. How much of the hunger bar is filled with apples? _____

2. How much of the hunger bar is filled with carrots? _____

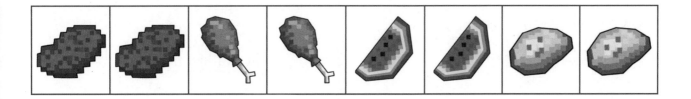

3. How much of the hunger bar has raw meat? _____

4. How much of the hunger bar has drumsticks? _____

5. How much of the hunger bar has melons? _____

6. How much of the hunger bar has potatoes? _____

EQUIVALENT FRACTIONS

I want two-eighths of a pie instead of one-fourth because 2 is more than 1.

Color and write an equivalent fraction.
The first one is done for you.

1.

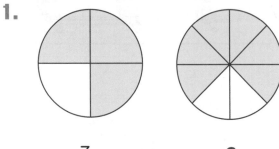

$$\frac{3}{4} = \frac{6}{8}$$

2.

$$\frac{2}{3} = \frac{}{6}$$

3.

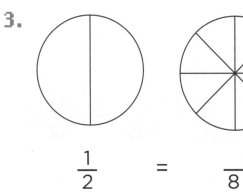

$$\frac{1}{2} = \frac{}{8}$$

4.

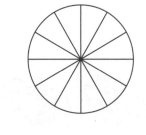

$$\frac{1}{4} = \frac{}{12}$$

5.

$$\frac{4}{6} = \frac{}{3}$$

6.

$$\frac{4}{16} = \frac{}{8}$$

7. Explain nitwit's mistake in his pie request.

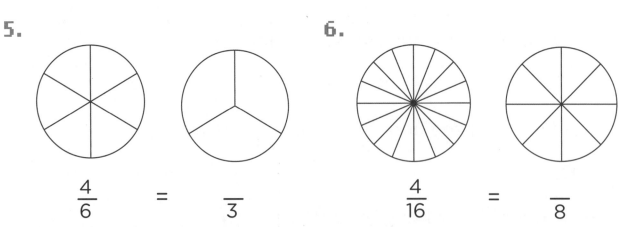

_____

_____

MORE EQUIVALENT FRACTIONS

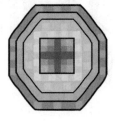

Color and write equivalent fractions.

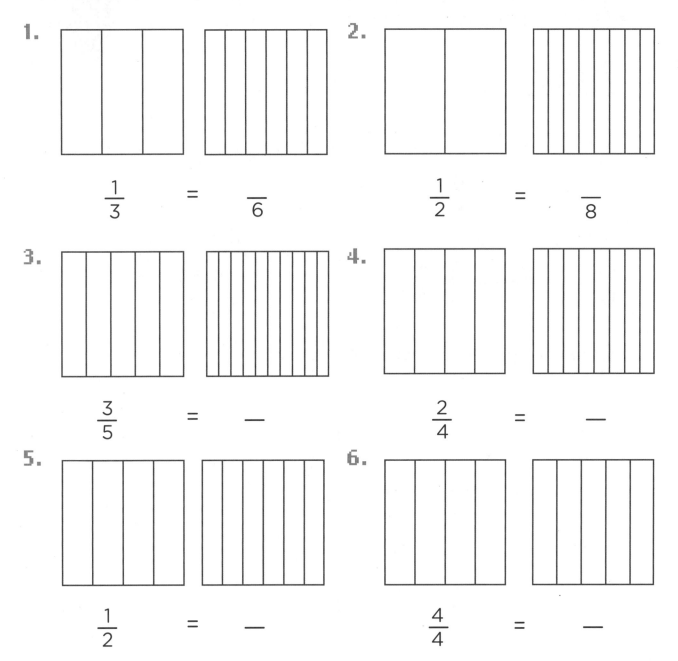

1.

$$\frac{1}{3} = \frac{}{6}$$

2.

$$\frac{1}{2} = \frac{}{8}$$

3.

$$\frac{3}{5} = \text{—}$$

4.

$$\frac{2}{4} = \text{—}$$

5.

$$\frac{1}{2} = \text{—}$$

6.

$$\frac{4}{4} = \text{—}$$

7. What's the pattern for finding equivalent fractions?

_____

ADDING FRACTIONS WITH LIKE DENOMINATORS

Color to add the fractions.
The first one is done for you.

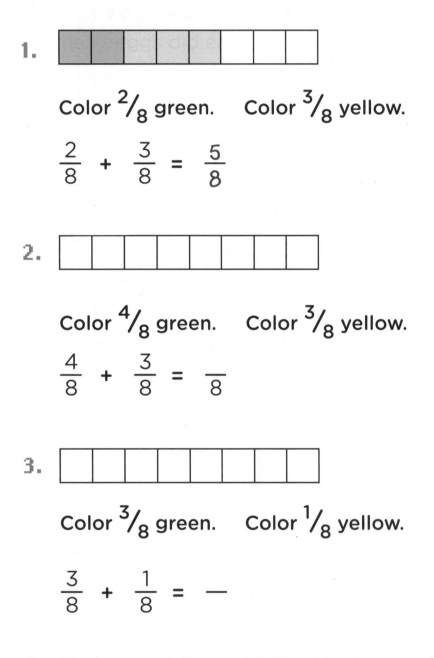

1.

Color $^2/_8$ green.   Color $^3/_8$ yellow.

$$\frac{2}{8} + \frac{3}{8} = \frac{5}{8}$$

2.

Color $^4/_8$ green.   Color $^3/_8$ yellow.

$$\frac{4}{8} + \frac{3}{8} = \frac{}{8}$$

3.

Color $^3/_8$ green.   Color $^1/_8$ yellow.

$$\frac{3}{8} + \frac{1}{8} = \text{---}$$

4. What is the pattern to add fractions? Use the words **numerator** and **denominator** in your response.

_____

SUBTRACTING FRACTIONS WITH LIKE DENOMINATORS

Color and cross out to subtract the fractions.
The first one is done for you.

1.
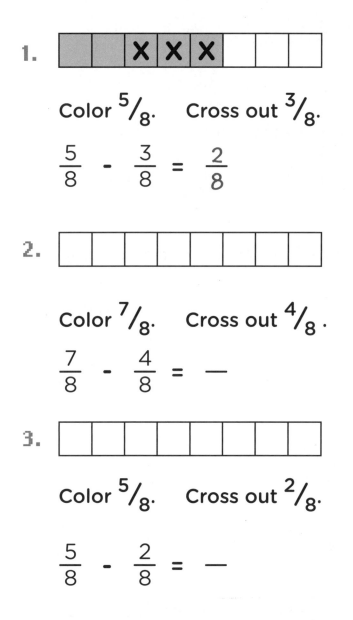

Color $^5/_8$.   Cross out $^3/_8$.

$$\frac{5}{8} - \frac{3}{8} = \frac{2}{8}$$

2.

Color $^7/_8$.   Cross out $^4/_8$.

$$\frac{7}{8} - \frac{4}{8} = \text{—}$$

3.

Color $^5/_8$.   Cross out $^2/_8$.

$$\frac{5}{8} - \frac{2}{8} = \text{—}$$

4. What is the pattern to subtracting fractions? Use the words **numerator** and **denominator** in your response.

_____

_____

IMPROPER AND MIXED FRACTIONS

An improper fraction has a numerator larger than the denominator.

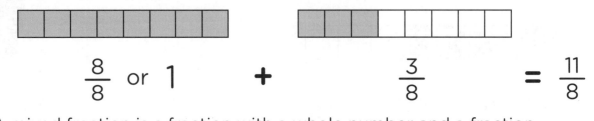

$$\frac{8}{8} \text{ or } 1 \quad + \quad \frac{3}{8} \quad = \quad \frac{11}{8}$$

A mixed fraction is a fraction with a whole number and a fraction.

$$\frac{11}{8} = 1\frac{3}{8}$$

Draw a line to match each improper fraction to its equivalent mixed number.

1. $^7/_5$

2. $^5/_3$

3. $^9/_8$

4. $^3/_2$

A. $1^2/_3$

B. $1^1/_8$

C. $1^2/_5$

D. $1^1/_2$

5. *The line between the numerator and the denominator means "divide." What is the pattern for finding the equivalent mixed number for an improper fraction?*

_____

FINDING PERIMETER

Find the perimeter of each letter. Each side of a square = 1 cm.

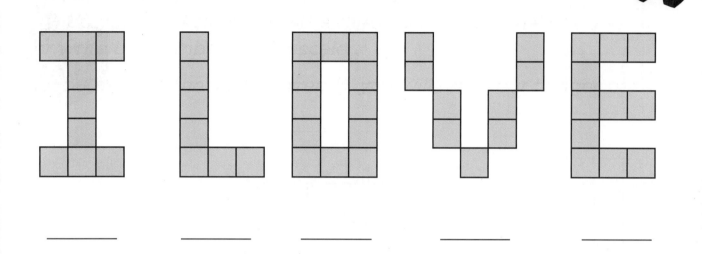

___   ___   ___   ___   ___

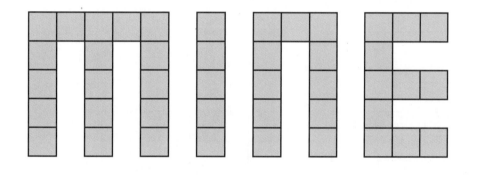

___   ___   ___   ___

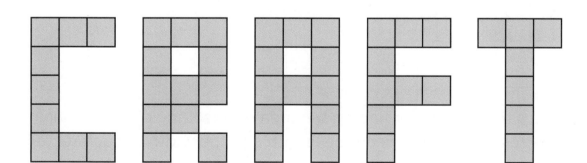

___   ___   ___   ___   ___

FINDING AREA

The area of the surface of this crafting table is 9.

Find the area of each rectangle.
Each side of a square = 1 cm.

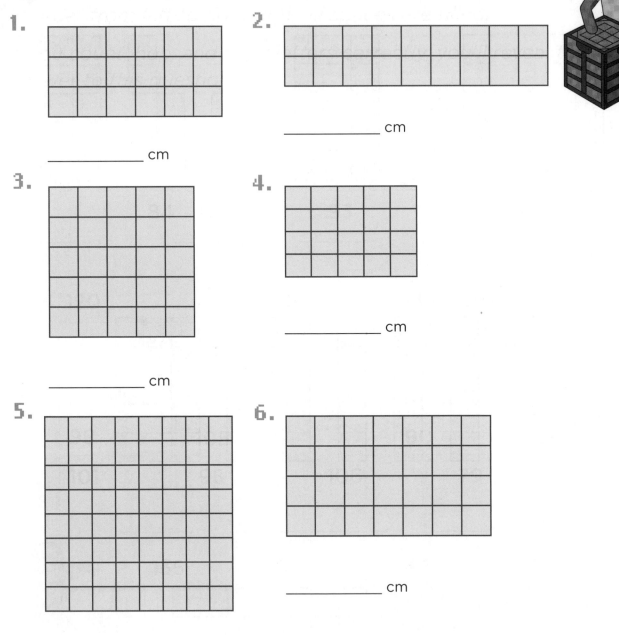

1.

_____ cm

2.

_____ cm

3.

_____ cm

4.

_____ cm

5.

_____ cm

6.

_____ cm

7. What is the pattern for finding the area of a rectangle? (**Hint:** Think about the relationship between the length and the width of each rectangle.)

_____

_____

READING FOR MINECRAFTERS

SYLLABLES

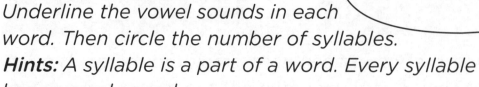

Underline the vowel sounds in each word. Then circle the number of syllables.

Hints: *A syllable is a part of a word. Every syllable has a vowel sound.*

Count how many times you move your mouth.

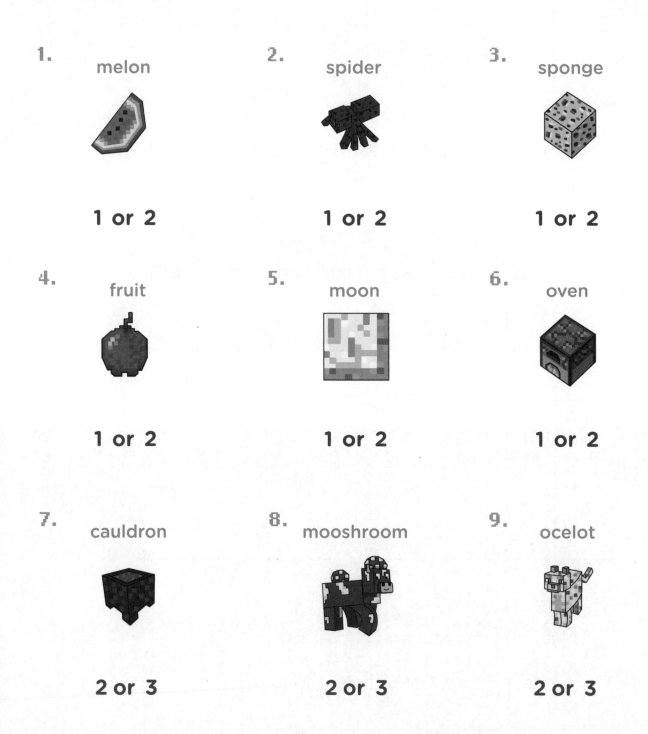

1. melon

1 or 2

2. spider

1 or 2

3. sponge

1 or 2

4. fruit

1 or 2

5. moon

1 or 2

6. oven

1 or 2

7. cauldron

2 or 3

8. mooshroom

2 or 3

9. ocelot

2 or 3

DIVIDING SYLLABLES

Draw a line between the syllables of each word.
The first one is done for you.

I am not
a ro/bot.

Hints:

- Divide between compound words.   **book/shelf**
- Prefixes and suffixes are syllables.   **creep/er**
- Divide after the long vowel.   **ro/bot**
- Divide after the consonant following a short vowel.   **Al/ex**

1.

glow/stone

2.

laughing

3.

spider

4.

apple

5.

lava

6.

crafted

7.

beetroot

8.

puffer

PREFIXES

Prefixes can be added before a word to change its meaning.

> The **un**opened chest is filled with gems.

re means again   ⟶   **re**view means to view again

dis means opposite of   ⟶   **dis**appear means the opposite of appear

un (or in) means not   ⟶   **un**opened means not opened

bi means two   ⟶   a **bi**cycle is a cycle with two wheels

tri means three   ⟶   a **tri**cycle is a cycle with three wheels

Underline the prefix. Draw a line to connect the word to its meaning.

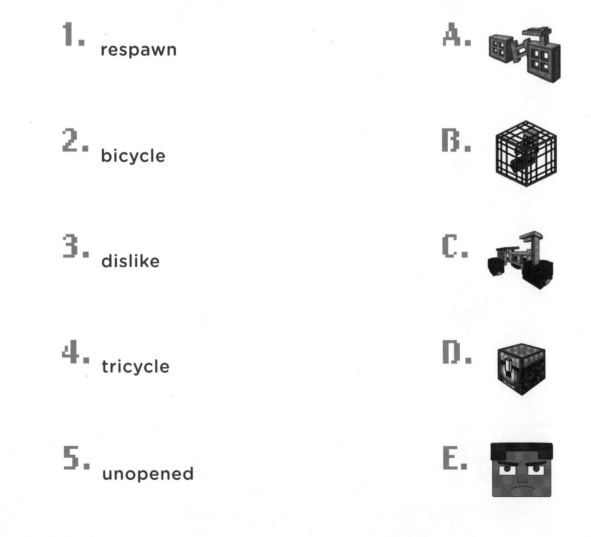

1. respawn

2. bicycle

3. dislike

4. tricycle

5. unopened

A.

B.

C.

D.

E.

PREFIXES

Complete the crossword puzzle with the words below or their prefixes.

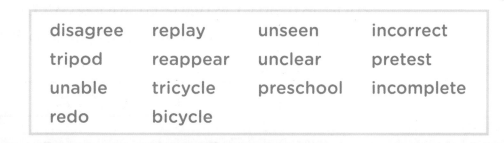

disagree	replay	unseen	incorrect
tripod	reappear	unclear	pretest
unable	tricycle	preschool	incomplete
redo	bicycle		

ACROSS

2 a cycle with three wheels

4 a test before a test

6 not complete

7 a prefix meaning the opposite of

8 not clear

10 to do again

11 a cycle with two wheels

13 not able

14 not seen

DOWN

1 to appear again

2 a stand with three legs

3 not correct

4 a school before school

5 to not agree

8 a prefix meaning not

9 to play again

11 a prefix meaning two

12 a prefix meaning to do again

FIND THE PREFIX

Read the sentence. Guess the meaning of the word in bold using the context clues and the prefix to help you.

1. There's a potion in Minecraft that makes a player **invisible**.

Meaning: _____

2. It's almost **impossible** to kill the Ender Dragon on your

first try.

Meaning: _____

3. Raw chorus fruit can be eaten, but popped chorus fruit

is **inedible**.

Meaning: _____

4. If minecart tracks are **disconnected**, your railway system

won't work.

Meaning: _____

5. If your parents are extremely **uninterested** in Minecraft,

you are not alone!

Meaning: _____

POLAR BEAR'S PREFIX CHALLENGE

Adding a prefix to the beginning of a root word can change the word's meaning. The prefixes dis, im, and in mean 'not' when added to the beginning of the words below. Write the new meaning of the word on the line. The first one is done for you.

	PREFIX		ROOT WORD		NEW WORD	NEW MEANING
1.	dis	+	like	=	dislike	not like
2.	dis	+	appear	=	_____	_____
3.	in	+	correct	=	_____	_____
4.	in	+	sane	=	_____	_____
5.	im	+	patient	=	_____	_____
6.	dis	+	agree	=	_____	_____

SUFFIXES

Suffixes can be added at the end of a word to change its meaning.

Here's a play**ful** pig.

able means able to	➡️	enjoy**able** means able to be enjoyed
en means to make	➡️	dark**en** means to make dark
ful means full of	➡️	beauti**ful** means full of beauty
less means without	➡️	fear**less** means without fear

Add a suffix to the word below the blank to complete the sentence.

1. The _____ pig chases after the
<u>play</u>

carrot on a stick.

2. Some potions will _____ mobs.
<u>weak</u>

3. A _____ ghast will sometimes
<u>care</u>

shoot itself.

4. Dying from a fall is _____ by
<u>avoid</u>

carrying a bucket of water.

SUFFIXES

Suffixes can be added at the end of a word to change its meaning.

er is added to compare two

est is added to compare more than two

Creeper is tall.

This creeper is tall**er**.

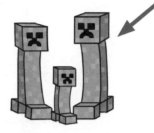

This creeper is the tall**est**.

*Add **er** or **est** to complete each sentence.*

1. The diamond sword is the sharp_____ of all swords.

2. The ocelot is fast_____ than pig.

3. Wither is dark_____ than skeleton.

4. The Arctic Biome is the cold_____ biome.

5. Iron golem is the kind_____ mob in the village.

6. Horse's tail is long_____ than goat's tail.

BUILDING WORDS

Add a prefix and a suffix to each word in the block. Then write what the word means.

PREFIXES	SUFFIXES
dis means opposite of	**ly** means like
un means not	**ful** means full of
mis means opposite of	**y** means like
im means not	**able** means able to be

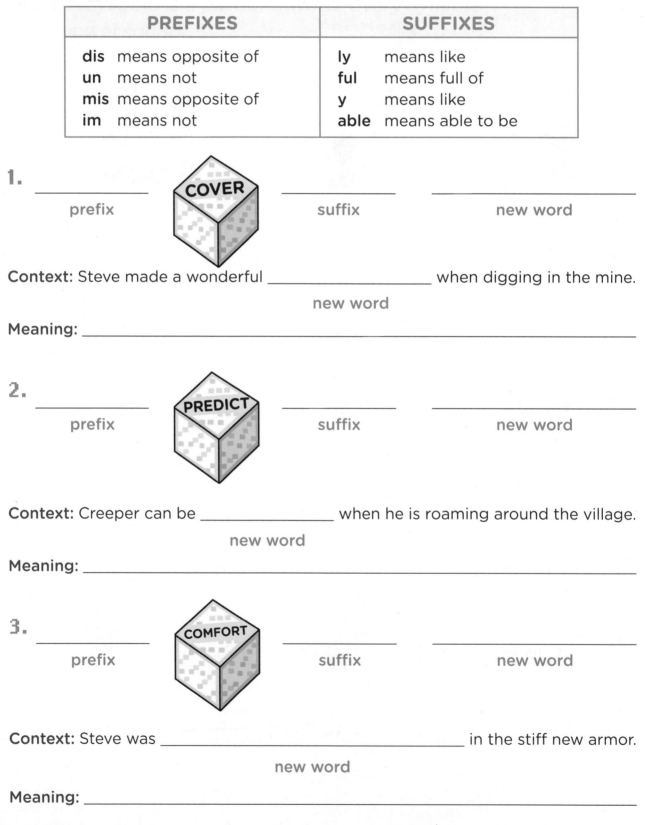

1. _____   COVER   _____   _____
        prefix   suffix   new word

Context: Steve made a wonderful _____ when digging in the mine.
                                             new word

Meaning: _____

2. _____   PREDICT   _____   _____
        prefix   suffix   new word

Context: Creeper can be _____ when he is roaming around the village.
                               new word

Meaning: _____

3. _____   COMFORT   _____   _____
        prefix   suffix   new word

Context: Steve was _____ in the stiff new armor.
                             new word

Meaning: _____

4. _____ AGREE _____ _____
      prefix   suffix   new word

Context: Pig can be very _____ when it is hungry.
                                        new word

Meaning: _____

5. _____ LUCK _____ _____
      prefix   suffix   new word

Context: Sometimes Steve feels _____ when the mob he battles wins.
                               new word

Meaning: _____

6. _____ PROPER _____ _____
      prefix   suffix   new word

Context: If a pig is treated _____ it will get angry.
                                   new word

Meaning: _____

7. _____ SUCCESS _____ _____
      prefix   suffix   new word

Context: Alex was _____ in her attempt to tame a creeper.
                          new word

Meaning: _____

CRAFTER'S CROSSWORD

When you join two words together, you can make a **compound word**, like butterfly. Use the list of compound words below and the word provided to fill in the rest of the crossword puzzle.

fireball   snowman   ~~watermelon~~

everybody   overworld   tripwire

                                    minecart

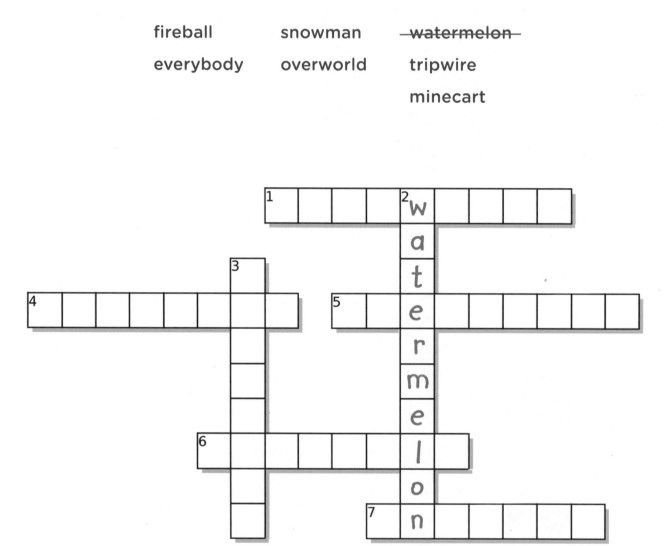

BUILDING COMPOUNDS

*What smaller word is missing from each **compound word**? Fill in the blanks to complete the word. Use the picture clues to help.*

1. Running through a cob_____ makes me go slower.

2. A day_____ sensor can automatically close your doors at night to keep mobs out.

3. Use a _____stone torch to power your next trap.

4. When you need a source of light, glow_____

blocks are very useful.

5. Eating _____ fish can be hazardous

to your health.

WHAT DOES IT MEAN?

Read each sentence. Use the context to figure out the meaning of the bolded word. Then circle the best meaning.

Hint: *Sometimes clues to a word's meaning can be found in the picture.*

1. The **shipwreck** was found in the deep ocean.

a sunken ship   a large new ship

2. Use the **enchanted** table to give weapons more power.

old   magical

3. Alex used the **shears** to get wool from sheep.

cutting tool   carrots

4. In **survival** mode, players must fight mobs to stay alive.

continuing to live   creating new building

LEARNING NEW WORDS

Complete the crossword puzzle using the words in the box. Use a dictionary if needed.

hostile	provocative	crafting	mob
biome	passive	block	dungeon
retaliate	aggressive		

ACROSS

3 to get back at

6 a cube

7 dark, dank room under a building

9 ready to attack

10 unfriendly

DOWN

1 making

2 causing anger or excitement

4 short for mobile

5 a community with similar plants and animals

8 non-threatening

CONTEXT CLUES

Read each sentence. Use the context to figure out the meaning of the bolded word. Then circle the best meaning.

1. A witch drinks **beneficial** potions as a protection against harm.

for the good   causing harm

2. The beacon projects a beam of light to **illuminate** the sky.

to darken   to light up

3. When hit by lightning, a pig **transforms** into a zombie pig.

changes   runs

4. A husk is a **variant** of a zombie that spawns in deserts.

friend   type

WORDS TO KNOW IN MINECRAFT

Find the Minecraft words in the puzzle. Look up the meaning of any word you don't know either online or in the dictionary.

mob	passive	hostile	potion	undead
variant	illuminate	beneficial	harmful	nether
creative	survival	aggressive	biome	

```
A P A S S I V E M O D B I
G E S U R V I V A L P H O
G H A R M F U L L T O N E
R O E P O T I O N S T V L
E S A B E N E F I C I A L
S T I L O I M E V N O R N
S I V B I O M E C E N I E
I L A I V M O B R A T A T
V E S U N D E A D S F N H
E C R E A T I V E T E T E
I L L U M I N A T E B E R
```

MULTIPLE MEANING WORDS

Some words have more than one meaning. Draw lines from each multiple meaning word to its meanings.

chest

an insect

1. bat

to move out of the way

a solid cube

2. pen

a basin for water

a flying mammal

3. ring

a circular band

the sound of a bell

4. fly

a tool to write

an animal that quacks

5. bark

to travel in the sky

to go below the water

6. block

a stick used to hit a ball

the outer layer of a tree

7. sink

to keep from passing

an animal enclosure

8. duck

the sound a dog makes

MULTIPLE MEANING WORDS

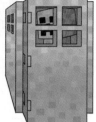

Read the sentence. Then write the letter of the meaning that matches the bold word.

1. If Steve is not careful, he will **trip** and fall into the lava. _____

    A. to stumble   **B.** a vacation

2. The diamond ore block is very **hard**. _____

    A. difficult   **B.** opposite of soft

3. The fireworks shot to the **right** of the building. _____

    A. correct   **B.** opposite of left

4. It is very **cold** in the Arctic Biome. _____

    A. a sickness   **B.** low temperature

5. It is **hard** to capture a creeper. _____

    A. difficult   **B.** opposite of soft

6. Steve hurt his **foot** when he kicked the block. _____

    A. a part of the body   **B.** 12 inches

SYNONYMS

*Synonyms are words with the same meaning.
Draw a line to match the synonyms.*

pretty beautiful

1. scared

2. delicious

3. shout

4. kind

5. mean

6. smart

7. sad

8. brave

A. nice

B. courageous

C. unhappy

D. cruel

E. afraid

F. yell

G. tasty

H. clever

ANTONYMS

Antonyms are words with opposite meanings.
Complete each sentence using an antonym of the
bold word.

short   tall

| fast | cold | closed | happy | harm |

1. Alex **opened** the chest, then _____ it.

2. Skeleton is **sad**, but Steve is _____ .

3. A pig is **slow**, but a cat is _____ .

4. Some potions **heal** and some potions _____ .

5. The Desert Biome is **hot**, but the Arctic Biome is _____ .

CLASSIFYING WORDS

Use the words in the box to label each group.
Then add one more to each group.

POTIONS	VILLAGERS	DROPS
HOSTILE MOBS	PLANTS	PASSIVE MOBS
BIOMES	FOODS	TOOLS AND WEAPONS

1.

cactus
bush
flower
tree

_____

2.

axe
bow and arrow
sword
hoe

_____

3.

creeper
zombie
witch
ghast

_____

4.

apple
porkchop
drumstick
bread

_____

5.

butcher
librarian
cleric
nitwit

_____

6.

cat
cow
pig
chicken

_____

7.

desert
ocean
jungle
snowy tundra

_____

8.

awkward
splash
strength
slowness

_____

9.

leather
raw beef
ink sac
blaze rod

_____

CLASSIFYING WORDS

Cross out the word that doesn't belong.
Then write the category.

1. granite   redstone   snow   diorite   andesite

Category: _____

2 spider   bat   dragon   bee   blaze

Category: _____

3. bed   chest   shelf   swing   rug

Category: _____

4. milk   water   diamond   potion   lava

Category: _____

5. chicken   llama   cow   goat   frog

Category: _____

6. clouds   sun   wind   rain   cobweb

Category: _____

7. fish   ghast   squid   shark   guardian

Category: _____

SEQUENCING

Read about how to tame a creeper. Then number the steps in the correct order.

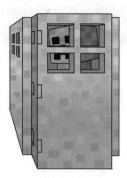

How to Tame a Creeper

Do you want to tame a creeper? First, get him to come to your creeper trap. He won't be happy in the trap. But that's okay. Just let him settle down. Put one red flower on one corner of the trap. Then put one yellow flower by the opposite corner of the trap. Then open the trap. The creeper will follow you. It won't explode or harm you. You now have a tamed creeper.

_____ You now have a tamed creeper.

_____ Open the trap.

_____ Let the creeper settle down.

_____ Put a yellow flower on the opposite corner of the trap.

_____ Get the creeper to come into the trap.

_____ Put a red flower on one corner of the trap.

_____ The creeper will follow you.

SEQUENCING

Read about how to build a snow golem.
Then number the steps in the correct order.

How to Build a Snow Golem

Brr! It's cold outside. Let's build a snow golem. First, you'll need a shovel, some snow, a crafting table, and a pumpkin head. Punch the snow with your shovel to make eight snowballs. Put two snowballs in each of the two bottom left squares of the crafting table. Then put two snowballs in each of the two middle left squares of the crafting table. This will make two snow blocks. Then put the pumpkin on top for the head. Snow golem is great at throwing snowballs at your enemy.

_____ Punch the snow with your shovel to make eight snowballs.

_____ Now you have two snow blocks.

_____ Then put two snowballs in each of the two middle left squares of the crafting table.

_____ First, you'll need a shovel, some snow, a crafting table, and a pumpkin head.

_____ Put a pumpkin on top for the head.

_____ Put two snowballs in each of the two bottom left squares of the crafting table.

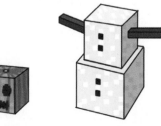

CAUSE AND EFFECT

Draw a line to match the cause with the effect.

Cause is the **why** something happens. Effect is **what** happens.

1. After a raid on a village,

2. When under water,

3. When lightning strikes,

4. After splashed with a potion of invisibility,

5. When a witch is killed,

6. When attacked by an evoker,

A. a witch will drink a healing potion.

B. a mob becomes invisible.

C. a villager will transform into a witch.

D. a witch will drink a potion of water breathing.

E. a witch celebrates by jumping and laughing.

F. it might drop spider eyes.

CAUSE AND EFFECT

Complete the missing parts of the chart to show cause and effect.

CAUSE	EFFECT
1. When lightning strikes a pig, 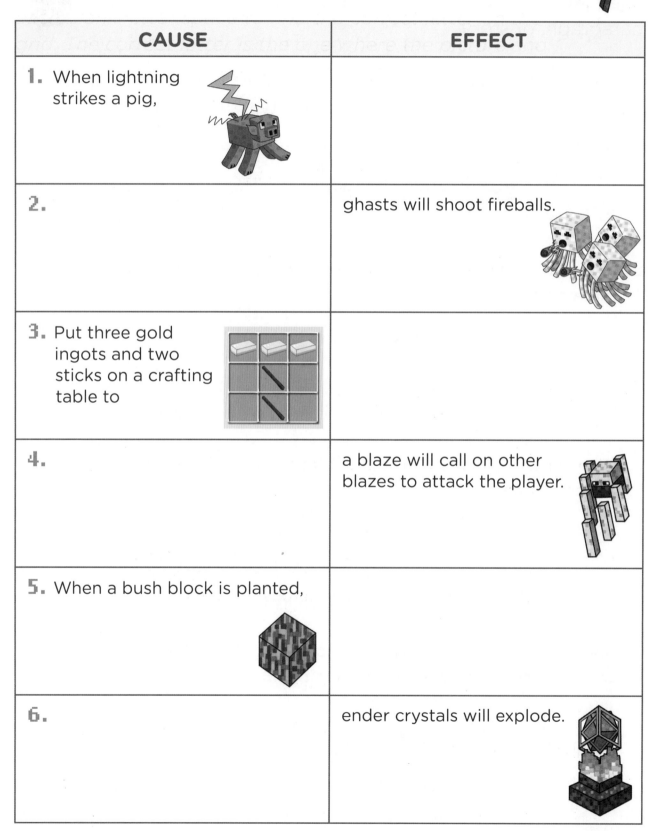	
2.	ghasts will shoot fireballs.
3. Put three gold ingots and two sticks on a crafting table to	
4.	a blaze will call on other blazes to attack the player.
5. When a bush block is planted,	
6.	ender crystals will explode.

MAIN IDEA

Circle the main idea of each sentence.

The **main idea** is the most important point of a sentence, paragraph, or story.

1. **When evokers are ready to attack, they raise their hands, showing different colors of particles for different types of attacks.**

   a. Evokers raise their hands when ready to attack.

   b. Evokers have many different types of attacks.

   c. Evokers always attack.

2. **When endermen are attacked, they shake and scream and make threatening sounds.**

   a. Endermen scream when they are ready to attack.

   b. Endermen are noisy mobs.

   c. Endermen scream and shake when they are attacked.

3. **When entering the End, watch out for the dangerous, flying ender dragon.**

   a. Be careful when entering the End because there are ender dragons.

   b. Ender dragons like to fly around the entrance to the End.

   c. Ender dragons are the most dangerous flying mob.

4. **Shulkers are box-shaped hostile mobs that hide in their shells in order to guard the treasure in the cities in the End.**

   a. Shulkers live in the End.

   b. Shulkers are box-shaped hostile mobs.

   c. Shulkers have lots of treasure.

MAIN IDEA AND SUPPORTING DETAILS

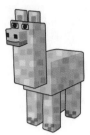

Read each paragraph. Write the main idea and two supporting details.

The **main idea** is the main point of the paragraph.
Supporting details provide information about the main idea.

1. Llamas are useful desert mobs. They are neutral mobs that can be tamed. They are strong mobs that can carry heavy loads. But be careful: If a llama is attacked, it will spit.

   Main Idea: _____

   Detail: _____

   Detail: _____

2. Husks are a type of zombie that lives in the desert. Unlike many zombies, husks do not burn in the sunlight. Like other zombies, they avoid cliffs and water. Husks look for turtle eggs. When they find the eggs, they trample them.

   Main Idea: _____

   Detail: _____

   Detail: _____

3. Desert biomes are large and lifeless. The surface is flat and sandy. Very few plants or animals live in the desert. There are very few hills in the desert.

   Main Idea: _____

   Detail: _____

   Detail: _____

MAKING INFERENCES

Read each sentence to infer the mob being described.

An **inference** is a conclusion reached, using evidence and reasoning.

1. I am a neutral mob that likes to climb on walls.

_____

2. I am a small mob that likes to fly and squeak loudly.

_____

3. I am a hostile mob that swims around and protects ocean monuments.

_____

4. I am a rare cow that lives in mushroom fields.

_____

5. I am a passive mob that moves on land and water and lays eggs in the sand.

_____

6. I am a passive mob found in the jungle. I hunt chickens and baby turtles. I like to sneak up on my prey.

_____

MAKING INFERENCES

Read the story. Answer the questions in complete sentences.

Steve was riding along in a minecart when a bug landed on his shoulder and stung him. "Ouch!" Steve yelled at the bug, and it flew away. Finally, Steve came to his destination. He took his pickaxe and began breaking away pieces of blocks to find what he needed for his project.

"Eureka!" shouted Steve. "This is just what I need!" He found two yellow ingots. "Now, I have everything I need for my project," Steve thought to himself and he headed home.

When he arrived home, he gathered a stick and his two yellow ingots and headed to his crafting table. He placed the two yellow ingots on the top two spaces in the middle of the table. He placed the stick on the bottom middle space. He waited and finally he was ready for battle.

1. Where did Steve go to find supplies for his project?

_____

2. Why did Steve yell "Ouch!"?

_____

3. Why did Steve shout "Eureka!"?

_____

4. What did Steve make?

_____

ZOMBIES VERSUS HUSKS

Read about zombies and husks. Underline the main idea of each paragraph with one line and each supporting detail with two lines.

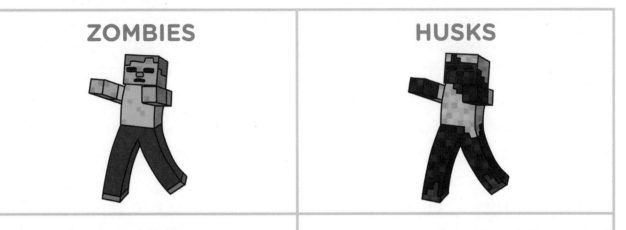

ZOMBIES	HUSKS
Zombies are a common mob in the Minecraft world. They often can be heard groaning as they wander around. They have a green block body like a creeper, but they have two arms and legs. They wear clothes similar to Steve.	Husks are variant zombies that live in the desert. They often can be heard groaning as they wander around. They have dark brown block bodies with two arms and legs. They wear a light brown shirt with dark brown pants.
Zombies are undead hostile mobs that attack players, villagers, iron golems, snow golems, and baby turtles. A zombie can spot a player from 40 blocks away. It will immediately chase after the player.	Husks are a hostile mob that attack players, villagers, iron golems, and baby turtles. They look for turtle eggs so they can stomp on them. They also cause hunger for several seconds when they attack.
Like other hostile mobs, zombies can be dangerous, but they are not indestructible. They burn in the daylight. They also avoid cliffs and lava and will sink in water. When zombies die, they drop rotten flesh. They might drop a carrot or potato. If a zombie is killed by a charged creeper, it will drop a zombie head.	Unlike zombies, husks do not burn in the sunlight. They avoid cliffs, water, and lava. When they die, they drop rotten flesh. They might also drop a carrot or a potato. If a husk drowns in water, it will turn back into a zombie, which then becomes a drowned. If a husk is killed by a charged creeper, it will not drop its head.

COMPARE AND CONTRAST

Use the information on page 196 to compare and contrast zombies and husks.

When you compare and contrast, using a Venn diagram, you write all the things they have in common in the center (intersecting) space. Then you write the things that are unique to each mob in the outside spaces.

ZOMBIES   HUSKS

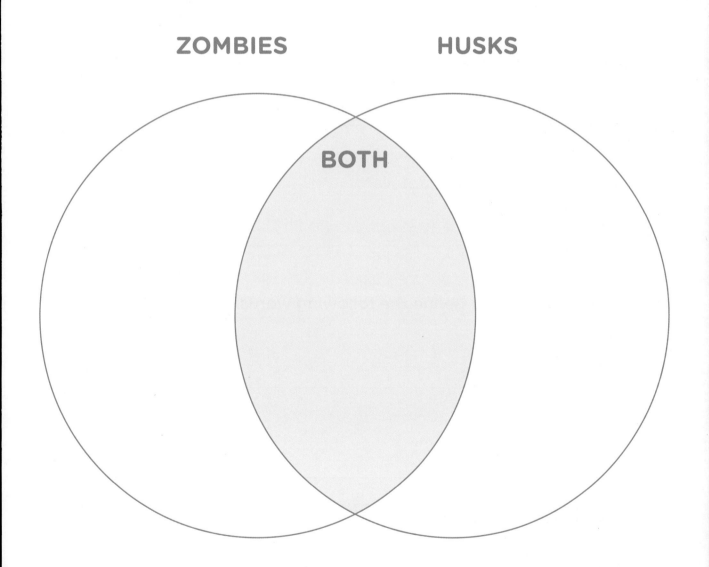

BOTH

DROWNED DETAILS

Read the paragraph. Answer the questions.

Drowned are underwater zombies. They walk and swim underwater. Sometimes they will **surface**. They may step on land but will quickly look for nearby water. Drowned are the only way for a player to get a trident. A trident is a weapon used in **melee** or close-range attacks. Drowned will also throw a trident at their **opponents** to kill it at a distance. If a villager is killed by a thrown trident, it will turn into a zombie villager.

1. **What is the main idea of the paragraph?**

   _____

2. **What are the supporting details?**

   _____

3. **Use context clues to define the following words.**

   a. surface

   _____

   b. melee

   _____

   c. opponent

   _____

SKELETON SKILLS

Read the paragraph. Answer the questions.

One early morning, skeleton was working out. He ran several flights of stairs and climbed ladders as quickly as he could. Then he timed himself running through a maze that he had created using some redstone blocks. He ran as quickly as he could through the maze. Next, he practiced **archery** by shooting over one hundred arrows. Not once did skeleton miss his target! After a short break, he practiced **strafing**, using spider as his target. He had spider stand on a block while he quickly circled spider, pretending to punch and dodge spider's punches. If he was up against a real enemy, those punches wouldn't be pretend. Skeleton is the best at strafing his opponents. Finally, skeleton ended his workout in the lake. Although he can't swim, he doesn't drown. He is able to continue shooting arrows underwater. The water does slow him down, so skeleton works on increasing his speed under water. Skeleton's **dedication** and hard work to develop his skills have made him one of the fiercest fighters in Minecraft.

1. What is the main idea of the paragraph?

_____

2. What are the supporting details?

_____

3. Use context clues to define the following words.

a. archery

_____

b. strafing

_____

c. dedication

_____

THE ANGRY WOLF

Read the fable. Answer the questions.

A **fable** is a short story that teaches a lesson. The lesson of the story is called a **moral**.

   One day an angry, growling wolf found a piece of beef. "I must hurry home to eat this meat, before anyone tries to steal it from me," growled the wolf to himself. Just then, creeper jumped out from behind a tree. The wolf growled loudly and showed its teeth. Creeper hissed and turned away. The wolf continued on his way. Then the wolf came to a river. Out of the corner of his eye, he saw another wolf in the river. He leaned over to growl at the wolf in the river, and the wolf in the river growled back. He opened his mouth to growl even louder and the meat fell into the water. It was then that he realized that the wolf in the river was actually his own reflection.

1. Who is the main character of the story?

   _____

2. Describe the main character.

   _____

   _____

3. What is the moral of the story?

   _____

   _____

BELLING THE ZOMBIE

Read the fable. Answer the questions.

One day the villagers met to discuss a problem. One villager stepped forward and said, "We must do something about all the zombie attacks." All the villagers shouted, "Yes!" The butcher shouted, "Let's chop them up." The witch shouted, "I'll make a potion." The nitwit started to speak but forgot what he wanted to say. Then the cleric stepped forward. "Let's tie a bell around each zombie's neck. Then we will hear the zombie coming from a distance and run to safety." "That's a great idea," shouted all the villagers. They began to jump with joy at finding a solution. Then nitwit stepped forward and said, "I wonder who will tie the bells around the zombies' necks." The villagers became silent. Slowly they each walked back to their own home.

1. Who are the characters in the story?

_____

2. What is the problem that the villagers had?

_____

3. What solution did they come up with?

_____

4. Why would the solution not work?

_____

5. What is the moral of the story?

_____

_____

THE UNUSUAL CREEPER

Read the story. Then answer the questions on the next page.

Once there was a creeper who spawned a rather unusual creeper. Unlike all the other green creepers with the delightful frown, this creeper was a pale purple color with a large smile. Not only was this creeper not green with a delightful frown, but also this young creeper was friendly. This was surprising to his parents, who had planned to spawn a young creeper who enjoyed attacking unwary players as much as they did. But like all good parents, they loved their young creeper for who he was. They still worried about how the other creepers would treat their young spawn.

Day after day, as the baby creeper continued to grow, he would listen to music and dance. This creeper was born to dance. Music and dance made him very happy. Instead of making the loud screeching noise like the other creepers, this young creeper had a voice like a singing bird.

"Oh dear," said his mother, "what will become of our spawn with this horrible sound? Why can't he screech like the rest of us?"

"He will find his way," said his father. "Everyone has a purpose, even a purple, smiling, singing creeper."

The father was right. When the young creeper grew up, he built a wonderful dance studio where he sang and danced. He taught other creepers to dance too. Everyone loved the dancing creeper, even the other creepers—well, as much as creepers can love.

THE UNUSUAL CREEPER

After reading the story on the previous page, answer the questions.

1. Who is the main character of the story?

_____

2. Circle the character traits that best describe the main character.

mean   friendly   hostile   sad   happy

passive   creative   angry   loving

3. Cite evidence from the story that supports the traits that you circled.

_____

_____

_____

4. Write how you are similar to or different from the unusual creeper.

_____

_____

_____

ZOMBIE INVASION

Read the story. Then answer the questions on the next page.

Early one morning while it was still dark, Steve entered a small village in the forest. The village had a sheer cliff on one side and a large lake on the other side. It was dark and quiet. No villagers could be seen. Suddenly, from the edge of the village, twenty zombies spawned. The undead hostile mobs moved into the village in groups of four.

When the zombies saw Steve, they began to attack. Steve shot arrows at them, but the zombies continued to attack. Nothing Steve did could stop the zombies. Then Steve saw the lake. He ran toward the lake and hid behind a tree. The zombies chased after Steve, but they lost him in the forest. Some zombies fell into the lake. The remaining zombies moaned loudly.

The villagers awoke. They began to panic. Some zombies turned to chase the villagers. Steve ran to save the villagers. When the zombies saw Steve, they began to chase him again. Steve ran toward the edge of the cliff and turned sharply to avoid falling over the cliff. Some of the zombies were not so lucky. They fell off the cliff. Steve battled the zombies until dawn. At dawn, some zombies ran into the forest. The other zombies were burned by the sunlight.

ZOMBIE INVASION

After reading the story on the previous page, answer the questions.

1. What is the setting of the story?

   _____

2. Describe the setting. Underline the evidence in the story that supports your description of the setting.

   _____

   _____

   _____

3. Would you like to be a character in this story? If yes, describe the character you would like to be and what you would do. If not, tell about a story you would like to be a character in.

   _____

   _____

   _____

   _____

IN THE JUNGLE

Read the story. Then complete the organizer on the next page.

Early one morning, Steve decide to explore the jungle. All around him he saw dark green plants and trees. The trees in the jungle grew tall. Some of them stood over thirty blocks high. At first glance, the jungle seemed quiet. Steve felt like he was alone.

Suddenly, Steve heard a loud squawk. He turned around to find a large, colorful parrot. Steve knew that parrots were helpful for spotting nearby mobs. So Steve tamed the parrot by feeding it some melon seeds he brought with him. The parrot perched on Steve's shoulder.

Together Steve and the parrot wandered further into the forest. "Roar," growled the parrot. This startled Steve. Again the parrot roared. Then Steve remembered that parrots imitated the sounds of nearby mobs. He recognized the roar—it was an ocelot.

Steve turned around slowly, looking for bright, shiny green eyes. Out of nowhere, an ocelot pounced. "Roar," it growled.

"I mean no harm. I'm just visiting the jungle," Steve explained. He tossed the ocelot some raw cod to gain its trust. Soon the ocelot trusted Steve.

Steve, the parrot, and the ocelot explored the jungle together until afternoon. Then Steve returned home. He enjoyed his adventure in the jungle.

IN THE JUNGLE

After reading the story on page 206, complete the graphic organizer.

TITLE OF STORY

CHARACTERS	SETTING

BEGINNING

MIDDLE

ENDING

FOLLOW YOUR OWN MINECRAFT ADVENTURE

Follow the arrows on the chart to choose an adventure.

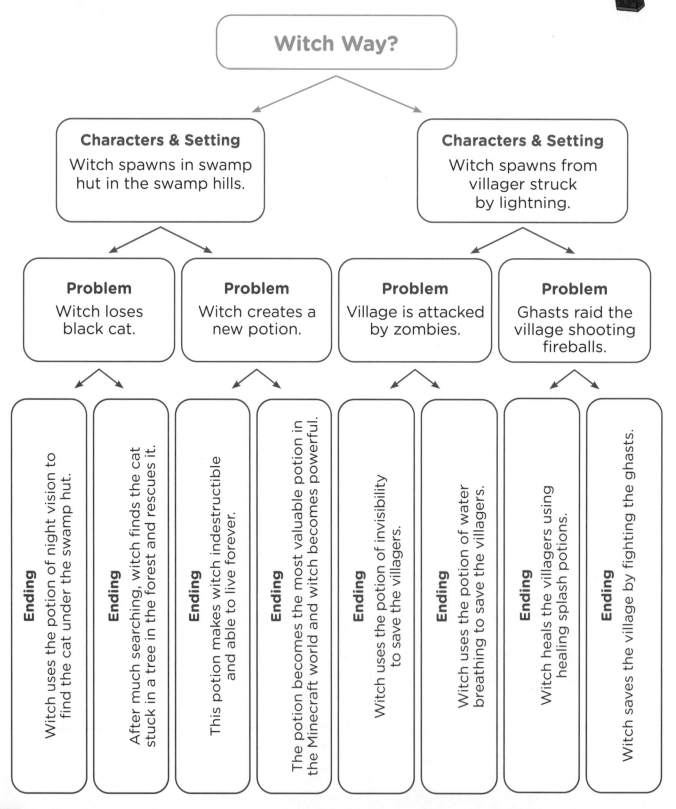

Witch Way?

Characters & Setting
Witch spawns in swamp hut in the swamp hills.

Characters & Setting
Witch spawns from villager struck by lightning.

Problem
Witch loses black cat.

Problem
Witch creates a new potion.

Problem
Village is attacked by zombies.

Problem
Ghasts raid the village shooting fireballs.

Ending
Witch uses the potion of night vision to find the cat under the swamp hut.

Ending
After much searching, witch finds the cat stuck in a tree in the forest and rescues it.

Ending
This potion makes witch indestructible and able to live forever.

Ending
The potion becomes the most valuable potion in the Minecraft world and witch becomes powerful.

Ending
Witch uses the potion of invisibility to save the villagers.

Ending
Witch uses the potion of water breathing to save the villagers.

Ending
Witch heals the villagers using healing splash potions.

Ending
Witch saves the village by fighting the ghasts.

WRITE YOUR OWN ADVENTURE

Use your choices from page 208 to write your adventure story.

WEATHER

Read about weather. Use the weather words to answer the riddles.

Air and water are all around us. The sun provides heat. It warms the air and water. Weather describes the air, water, and heat that surround us. When we talk about the weather, we use words like sunny, rainy, windy, snowy, hot, and cold. Weather changes daily. Weather is different in different places. Weather is different in different seasons. Weather affects how we dress and what we do. Weather affects how we live.

| wind | cloud | rain | hail | snowflake | thunder | lightning | temperature |

1. I clap without any hands. What am I? _____

2. I can be a gentle breeze or a strong gust. What am I?

   _____

3. I am little balls of frozen snow. What am I? _____

4. I may be flaky, but I am one of a kind. What am I?

   _____

5. I drop from way up high. When the sun shines I make a bow across

   the sky. What am I? _____

6. I light up the sky on a dark stormy day. What am I?

   _____

7. I rise up and down but never move. What am I?

   _____

8. I may look fluffy like a pillow but I am all wet. What am I?

   _____

CLOUDS

Read about clouds in the real world. Tell the area and perimeter of the Minecraft clouds. Each side of a square = 1 cm.

When the sun heats the water, the water rises and forms clouds. Clouds are made of small water droplets. Clouds form when the temperature in the sky cools. There are three main types of clouds—cirrus, stratus, and cumulus. Cirrus clouds are high and thin. Stratus clouds look like flat sheets. They cover most of the sky. They usually bring rain. Cumulus clouds look soft and puffy. White cumulus clouds mean good weather. Gray cumulus clouds mean rain.

1.

Area: _____ cm

Perimeter: _____ cm

2.

Area: _____ cm

Perimeter: _____ cm

3.

Area: _____ cm

Perimeter: _____ cm

4.

Area: _____ cm

Perimeter: _____ cm

PRECIPITATION

Read about precipitation. Complete the acrostic puzzle with words about precipitation.

Clouds form from water that evaporates from the earth. When the temperature of a **cloud** cools, it creates precipitation. **Precipitation** is water that falls from the clouds. Waterdrops are called **rain**. When clouds get even colder, the waterdrops turn to **ice** or **snow**. Sometimes rain will freeze as it falls. This is called **sleet**. Sometimes when snow falls, it collects more water on the way down. The wind carries the snow back up to the clouds, where it freezes again. This forms ice balls or **hail**.

MINECRAFT FUN FACT

Weather in Minecraft changes only for a few seconds. Then it goes back to normal.

WEATHER FORECASTING

Look at the forecast for weather in the Minecraft world. Use the key to answer the questions.

Minecraft Weather Forecast

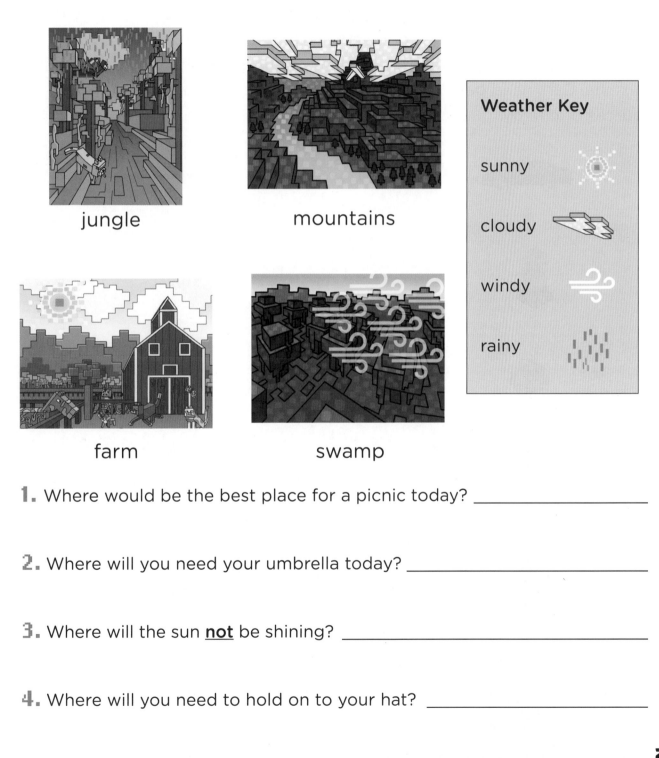

jungle

mountains

farm

swamp

Weather Key

sunny

cloudy

windy

rainy

1. Where would be the best place for a picnic today? _____

2. Where will you need your umbrella today? _____

3. Where will the sun **not** be shining? _____

4. Where will you need to hold on to your hat? _____

ENERGY

Read about energy. Draw a line to match each picture to its energy source.

I get energy from cake!

Energy is how things move and change. Plants need energy to grow. People need energy to move. Machines need energy to work. There are many types of energy. Some energy is found in nature. Some energy is made by humans. The sun is one energy source. It provides plants the energy to grow. People need food to make energy. Lights need electricity to shine. Cars need gasoline or other fuel to run. Heat and wind are other sources of energy.

1.

2.

3.

4.

5.

6.

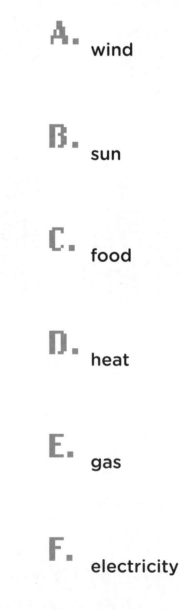

A. wind

B. sun

C. food

D. heat

E. gas

F. electricity

HEAT ENERGY

Read about heat energy. Tell about the heat energy in each picture.

Heat energy is all around us. The sun produces heat energy. The sun keeps us warm. Heat energy causes water to move through the water cycle. We also use heat energy to cook. Fire is a source of heat energy. Fire creates heat to warm us. Fire uses heat to make things melt.

1. How does the torch use heat energy?

_____

2. How does rabbit stew use heat energy?

_____

3. How does the thistle use heat energy?

_____

4. How does nitwit use heat energy?

_____

5. What will happen to snow golem if it heats up?

_____

6. What will happen if zombie falls in lava?

LIGHT ENERGY

Read about light energy. Then answer the questions by circling yes or no.

Light is a source of energy. The sun, fire, and electricity all produce light. Light energy travels in waves. It helps us see. It produces colors. Light cannot pass through opaque objects. It can only pass through transparent objects. When light is blocked, it makes a shadow.

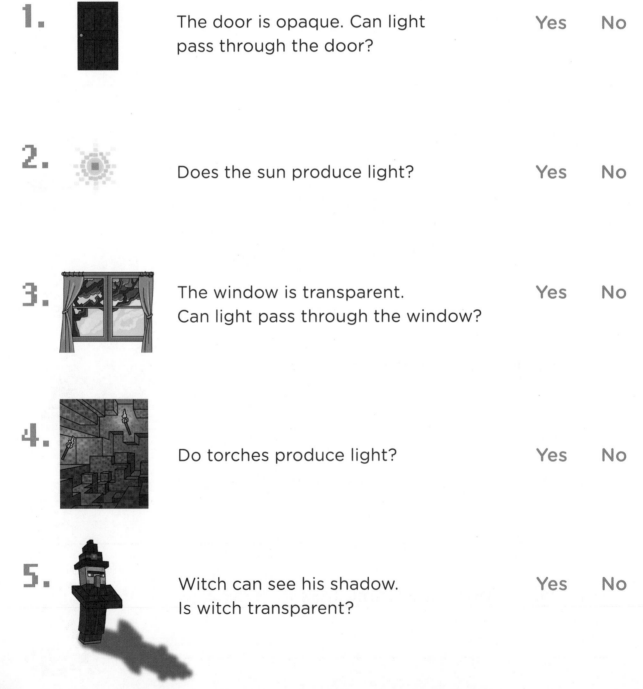

1. The door is opaque. Can light pass through the door?

Yes   No

2. Does the sun produce light?

Yes   No

3. The window is transparent. Can light pass through the window?

Yes   No

4. Do torches produce light?

Yes   No

5. Witch can see his shadow. Is witch transparent?

Yes   No

SOUND ENERGY

Read about sound energy. Draw some sound waves.

I like to make loud SSSSSSounds!

Sound is a type of energy caused by vibration. Sounds moves through the air in waves. Loud sounds have more energy and vibrate faster than quiet sounds. Pitch is how high or low a sound is.

This wave shows a high pitch.

This wave shows a low pitch.

This wave shows a loud sound.

This wave shows a quiet sound.

1. Draw a sound wave that shows Alex whispering to pig.

2. Draw a sound wave that shows ghast screeching.

FORCE AND MOTION

Read about force and motion. Answer the questions. Write to explain your answer.

Objects stay at rest until a force causes them to move. Objects can be pushed or pulled. It is easier to pull a heavy object because there is less friction. The heavier an object is, the more force it takes to move it. More force makes objects move faster.

1. Which object would take more force to move?

_____

2. Would it be easier to push or pull a cow?

_____

3. Which object would you rather have fall on your head?

_____

4. Will going uphill or downhill make the minecart go faster?

_____

FORCE AND MOTION

Read more about force and motion. Answer the questions. Write to explain your answer.

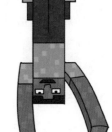

It takes force to slow or stop a moving object. It also takes force to change the direction that an object is moving in. Friction is a force that slows objects down. Gravity is a force that pulls objects to the ground.

1. Describe a force that Alex might use to stop a spider crawling on her wall. _____

2. Describe a force that brings a ball tossed in the air back to the ground.

_____

3. Skeleton throws bones on the track. Describe how the bones will act as a force against Steve's cart.

_____

_____

4. Alex and Steve are riding downhill in their minecarts toward each other. Explain what will happen.

_____

_____

COMPARE AND CONTRAST

Read about wither and wither skeleton. Then, use the Venn diagram to compare and contrast them.

Hints: Things that describe only wither go in the left circle.

Things that describe only wither skeleton go in the right circle.

Things that describe both wither and wither skeleton go in the middle.

Wither has three heads. Wither likes to shoot explosive skulls at players. It turns a player's heart black. When wither dies, it drops a nether star. Wither is immune to fire, lava, and drowning. Wither skeleton is an underworld skeleton. It will attack with its stone sword. It also will turn a player's heart black. When a wither skeleton dies, it may drop its sword, bones, or coal. It is immune to fire and lava.

WITHER

WITHER SKELETON

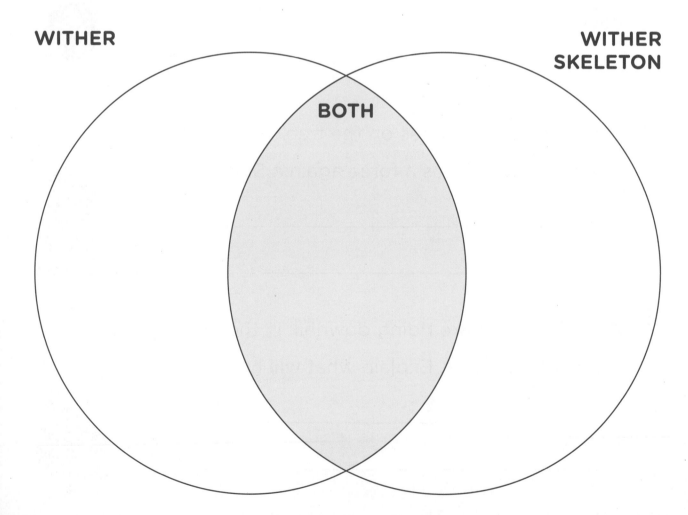

BOTH

WRITING FOR MINECRAFTERS

SENTENCES

A **sentence** is a group of words that tells a complete thought. All sentences begin with a **capital letter**. A statement ends with a **period**. A sentence includes a **noun**, a **verb**, and sometimes an **adjective** or **adverb**.

ADVERB	VERB	ADJECTIVE	NOUN
describes a verb, sometimes ends in "ly"	an action word, like *run*	a describing word, like *scary*	a person, place, or thing, like *creeper*

Read the sentences on the opposite page and follow the instructions below.

- Draw a triangle around the **capital letter** that begins the sentence.

- Circle the **noun** (there may be more than one).

- Underline the **verb**.

- Draw a rectangle around the **adjective** and **adverbs**.

- Draw a square around the **period** that ends the sentence.

1.  The scary wither angrily attacks a player.

2.  A dizzy zombie groans loudly.

3.  A skeleton secretly fires poison arrows.

4.  Quickly hide your loot in a large chest.

5. 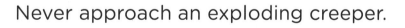 Never approach an exploding creeper.

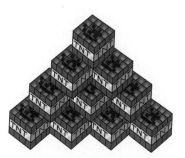 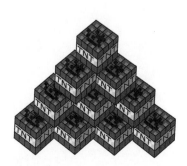

SUBJECT AND VERB

Connect the words to make a sentence.
The first one is done for you.

1.

Guardian   Squids

swim   swims

up.   down.

2.

Horses   Steve

eat   eats

cake.   carrots.

3.

Alex   Baby zombies

ride   rides

a pig.   chickens.

4.

Creepers   Creeper

explodes   dance

to the music.   on the player.

SUBJECT AND VERB

Write the correct verb on the line.

1. Villagers _____ passive
non-player characters.

is /are

2. Baby villagers _____ adults after
20 minutes.

become / becomes

3. A villager _____ clothes that show
his job.

wear / wears

4. Nitwits _____ not have jobs.

do / does

5. Players _____ with villagers.

trade / trades

6. Villagers _____ emeralds.

like / likes

VERB AGREEMENT

*Verbs have to agree with their subject. Witches **brew** potion, but a single witch **brews** potion. Look at the sentences below. Choose the best verb from the word box and write it on the line. Make sure it agrees with the subject.*

| build | teleport | attack | swim | shoot |

1. Steve _____ a sword on his crafting table.

2. The player _____ the spider with his sword.

3. When a skeleton _____ arrows at you, it's best to run.

4. Endermen will _____ toward you if you make eye contact.

5. A dolphin usually _____ with other dolphins.

VERB AGREEMENT

(Continued from previous page)

*Fix each sentence by changing the **verb** to match the subject. The first one is done for you.*

1.
   brings
   Alex ~~bring~~ her golden sword with her to the End.

2.
   To make your flowers grows, place them in bonemeal.

3.
   The Enderman teleport over to Steve.

4.
   The players makes fishing rods from sticks and string.

5.
   The witch throw a splash potion.

6.
   The skeleton shoot many arrows.

7.
   The zombie prefer to live in the dark.

8.
   The jungle biomes has a lot of trees.

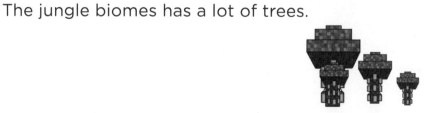

COMPOUND SUBJECTS

Combine the compound subjects and write the new sentence. The first one is done for you.

Compound subjects are two subjects that have the same predicate. You can combine compound subjects into one sentence using the conjunction *and.* Watch the verbs!

1. Creeper is a hostile mob. Witch is a hostile mob.

   <u>Creeper and witch are hostile mobs.</u>

2. Steve likes to mine for diamonds. Alex likes to mine for diamonds.

   _____

3. Ender dragon flies. Blaze flies.

   _____

4. The potion of invisibility has positive effects. The potion of healing has positive effects.

   _____

5. The ocelot can be found in the jungle. The parrot can be found in the jungle.

   _____

COMPOUND PREDICATES

Combine the compound predicates and write the new sentence. The first one is done for you.

Compound predicates are two predicates that have the same subject. You can combine compound predicates into one sentence using the conjunction *and*.

1. Steve likes to fish in the lake. Steve likes to explore in the forest.

   <u>Steve likes to fish in the lake and explore in the forest.</u>

2. Witch lives in the village. Witch makes many potions.

   _____

3. Skeleton chased the player. Skeleton shot the player with his arrow.

   _____

4. Spider crawled up the wall. Spider crawled through the cobweb.

   _____

5. Nitwit has no job. Nitwit wanders through the village.

   _____

POSSESSIVE (SINGULAR)

*Fix the sentences below to make the noun **possessive.***
The first one is done for you.

> A possessive noun shows ownership. Add an apostrophe and s ('s) to form the possessive of most singular nouns.
>
> The computer of the gamer is fast. The **gamer's** computer is fast.

1. The arrow of the skeleton is sharp.

<u>The skeleton's arrow is sharp.</u>

2. The shirt of Alex is green.

_____

3. The magnet of Steve is strong.

_____

4. The hut of the witch is in the forest.

_____

5. The mask of the thief is black.

_____

6. The clothes of the zombie are ripped.

_____

POSSESSIVE (PLURAL)

Write the **possessive** form of each plural noun on the line.
The first one is done for you.

A possessive noun shows ownership. To make a regular plural noun possessive, add an apostrophe (') after the s.

The faces of the creepers are green.   The creepers' faces are green.

To make an irregular plural noun possessive, add an apostrophe and s ('s).

The books of the children are heavy.   The children's books are heavy.

1. The petals of the flowers

The flowers' petals _____

2. The potions of the witches

_____

3. The spots of the mushrooms

_____

4. The wool of the sheep

_____

5. The city of the people

_____

QUOTE ME

Add quotation marks where they belong in the sentences below.

1. Do you have anything to trade? asked the villager.

2. Alex ran from the creeper yelling, It's gonna blow!

3. Steve, said Alex, I think it's time to explore the Nether.

4. After throwing her splash potion, the witch yelled, I'll get you next time.

5. This is bad, said the zombie when it noticed the sun coming out.

Write your own quotation below.

_____

_____

_____

QUOTATION MARKS

Circle the places where the quotation marks are missing or in the wrong place. Put them in the correct place.

1. What a beautiful emerald," said Steve.

2. "Let's go looking" for tonight's dinner, said Alex.

3. "Quick! Get your bow and arrow"! Steve yelled.

4. "I want to be a chicken jockey when I grow up, said the baby zombie."

5. "I have a new diamond chest plate, Steve told Alex.

COMMONLY CONFUSED WORDS

Some words sound the same but are spelled differently. Choose the correct word from the box to complete the sentence. Some words may be used more than once.

their	they're	there

1. Alex and Steve laugh at _____ joke.

2. The brewing stand is over _____ .

3. The witches will use eye of Ender in _____ potion.

4. Even when zombies travel in a mob, _____ very slow.

5. The arctic fox blends in well with _____ surroundings.

its	it's

6. _____ important to water your crops every day.

7. When TNT explodes, _____ noisy.

to	two	too

8. The _____ creepers are dancing.

9. The health meter can never be _____ full.

10. The iron golem hands a poppy _____ the villager.

11. You need _____ tripwire hooks _____ make a tripwire trap.

loose	lose

12. The animals have gotten _____ from their pen.

13. Make a compass so you do not _____ your way in Minecraft.

MORE COMMONLY CONFUSED WORDS

Choose the correct word from the box to complete the sentence.

good – adjective used to describe a noun **well** – adverb used to describe a verb

1. Pig isn't feeling _____ .

2. Skeleton is _____ .

your – possessive pronoun   **you're** – contraction for you are

3. Is Enderman _____ favorite mob?

4. "_____ my favorite," Alex said to pig.

than – used to compare   **then** – used to show passage of time

5. The arctic fox blends in better _____ pig.

6. After you plant your crops, _____ you water them every day.

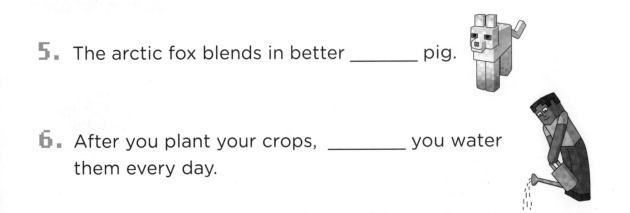

COMMONLY CONFUSED WORDS

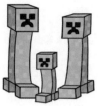

Choose the correct word from the box to complete the sentence.

this – adjective to describe one thing that is close	**that** – adjective to describe one thing at a distance
these – adjective to describe more than one thing that is close	**those** – adjective to describe more than one thing at a distance

7. Alex looked at the carrot in her hand. "_____ carrot will help me tame pig," thought Alex.

8. Steve watched his friends at the next farm. He thought, "_____ cow is being stubborn."

9. "_____ ghasts are attacking me!" shouted Alex.

10. "Which eggs did chicken lay?" asked Steve. Alex pointed to the far side of the barn. "Chicken just laid _____ eggs," she said.

accept – to receive	**except** – to exclude

11. "Will you _____ this flower?" asked iron golem.

12. Most mobs leave drops when they are killed, _____ ocelot.

ADDING ADJECTIVES

Rewrite the sentences adding descriptive adjectives.

An **adjective** can tell how many (nine, two, hundreds), can tell what color (green, red, yellow), and can provide physical descriptions (tall, short, cute). Some adjectives used to describe Minecraft mobs are in the box. Look up the meaning of the ones you don't know. Feel free to use your own words. Remember: adjectives only describe nouns.

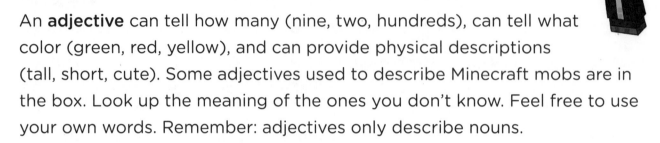

ADJECTIVES						
magical	hostile	passive	fierce	scary	slimy	raging
deadly	interesting	rare	common	variant	notorious	
charged	undead	zombified	beautiful			

1. Creeper is a mob.

_____

2. Steve found a gem in the mine.

_____

3. The ocelot stalked the player.

_____

4. Evoker cast spells.

_____

5. The spider climbed the wall.

_____

6. The beacon beamed light into the sky.

_____

ADDING ADVERBS

Underline the verb in each sentence. Then circle the adverb.

Verbs are action words. **Adverbs** describe verbs. Adverbs tell how, when, or where the action takes place.

1. The zombie ran quickly away from the lava.

2. Alex fought bravely against the ender dragon.

3. Steve carefully crafted the new sword.

4. Yesterday the sun shone brightly in the Minecraft world.

5. Steve and Alex laughed loudly at the joke.

6. The whirlwind spun rapidly across the desert.

7. Everywhere Steve looked, zombies marched randomly around the village.

8. The cocoa tree grew tall and straight in the jungle.

ADDING DETAILS

*Rewrite each sentence, adding details to make
the sentence more interesting.*

Adjectives
(describe people and things)

dark	heavy	enormous
creepy	tall	tiny
cute	strong	long	windy

Adverbs
(describe actions)

slowly	lazily
wildly	mightily
quickly	

Prepositional Phrases

under the trees	of heavy gems	over the mountain
by the river	down the mountain	in a cave

1. Some mountains have caves.

_____

2. The llama lives in the mountains.

_____

3. Llamas carry chests.

_____

4. Some rivers run.

_____

ADDING DETAILS

Add details to the sentences to tell how, when, and where. Use words from the box or your own words.

How	When	Where
slowly	at night	in the jungle
loudly	after eating	in the Arctic
silently	early	by the cave
quickly	soon	in the ocean
sadly	always	over the city

1. The parrot squawks.

_____

2. The ship sank.

_____

3. The wolf jockey rode the wolf.

_____

4. The dragon flew.

_____

SENSORY DETAIL

Use lots of detail to make your writing more interesting and fun to read. Finish the sentences below with sensory detail. You'll need to first imagine what each item feels, tastes, looks, sounds, or smells like.

1. The zombie sounded _____

_____.

2. She grabbed the Ender pearl, and it felt _____

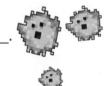

_____ in her hand.

3. The pufferfish tasted _____.

4. Up close, the portal looked _____

_____.

5. The sound the pickaxe made as it hit the redstone ore was

_____.

SENSORY DETAILS

In writing, **sensory details** describe what a character sees, hears, smells, touches, and tastes. Look at the picture of a diver exploring an underwater shipwreck. Write a paragraph describing the diver's experience using lots of sensory detail.

_____

_____

_____

_____

_____

_____

_____

_____

_____

_____

_____

RELATIVE PRONOUNS

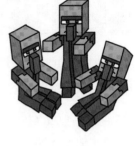

A **relative pronoun** refers back to a noun that was already mentioned. Some examples of relative pronouns are: **that, which, who, whose,** and **whom.** Circle the relative pronoun in the sentences below.

1. Minecraft is the video game that most kids play.

2. Minecraft, which can be played in Survival Mode

or Creative Mode, is exciting.

3. Pigs are animals that can be tamed with a carrot.

4. Is that the mob that chased you?

5. The Enderman that finishes first wins the race.

6. The player who built the snow golem is very clever.

7. That's the chest which holds her armor.

8. That's the player whose armor is gold.

244

MORE RELATIVE PRONOUNS

Fill in the blank with a word from the box. Who *and* whose *refer to people.* That *refers to things. Underline the person or thing that the relative pronoun refers to. The first one is done for you.*

who	whose	that

1. Alex is the girl _____**who**_____ is hugging the pig.

2. The diamond _____ Alex is holding is shiny.

3. The diamond sword _____ Steve made is very sharp.

4. The witch _____ potion I used is wearing a purple robe.

5. The villager _____ grew the glistening melon is a good farmer.

PRESENT PROGRESSIVE TENSE

Progressive verb tenses are used to talk about an action that is in progress. This can be something that is happening now, was happening in the past, or will be happening in the future.

The **present progressive tense** tells about something happening now. It uses the helping verb **is, am,** or **are** and the **-ing** form of the verb.

Example: The horse **is eating** a carrot.   The skeletons **are walking**.

Change the sentences below from the present tense to the present progressive tense. The first one is done for you.

1. Steve mines for diamonds.

   <u>Steve is mining for diamonds.</u>

2. The villagers wait to trade.

   _____

3. Alex rides in her minecart.

   _____

4. The chicken lays eggs.

   _____

5. I play Minecraft with my friends.

   _____

PAST PROGRESSIVE TENSE

The **past progressive tense** tells about something that was happening in the past. It uses the helping verb was or were and the –ing form of the verb. Usually the past progressive tense talks about an action that happened in the middle of another action.

Example: The zombie **was laughing** when he fell into the lava pit.
The skeletons **were groaning** as they walked.

Change the sentences below from the past tense to the past progressive tense. The first one is done for you.

1. The skeleton ran as it shot its arrows.

   <u>The skeleton was running as it shot its arrows.</u>

2. The ghasts threw fireballs as they attacked.

   _____

3. Alex smiled as she crafted a golden sword.

   _____

4. The creeper plotted revenge while he was in the trap.

   _____

5. The torches lit the way as Steve entered the cave.

   _____

FUTURE PROGRESSIVE TENSE

The **future progressive tense** tells about something that will be happening in the future. It uses the helping verb **will be** and the **-ing** form of the verb. Usually the future progressive tense talks about an action that will be ongoing.

Example: The horse **will be eating a carrot.**   The skeletons **will be walking.**

Change the sentences below from the present tense to the future progressive tense. The first one is done for you.

1. Alex fights the Ender dragon tomorrow.

   <u>Alex will be fighting the Ender dragon tomorrow.</u>

2. The bat flies tonight.

   _____

3. I look for some blaze powder to make a potion.

   _____

4. The ghast shoots fireballs at the player.

   _____

5. Steve crafts a diamond sword next week.

   _____

MODAL AUXILIARY VERBS

Modal auxiliary verbs show that something is possible or necessary. Verbs that show something is possible include: **can, may,** and **might**. Verbs that show something is necessary include: **must** and **has to/have to**.

Underline the modal auxiliary verbs in the sentences below. On the line, write whether the verb shows that something is possible (P) or necessary (N). The first one is done for you.

P — **1.** The bee <u>might</u> sting you.

_____ **2.** The carrot must hang on the fishing rod.

_____ **3.** An exploding creeper can damage a player.

_____ **4.** Alex has to collect eight diamonds to make a chestplate.

_____ **5.** Steve may mine until dinnertime.

_____ **6.** The witch might brew a potion later.

WRITE ABOUT A TOPIC

*Which is your favorite way to play Minecraft, in Survival, Creative, Adventure, Spectator, or Hardcore mode? Explain why. Be sure to include **definitions** for tricky words that readers might not know. Add plenty of **details** to support your ideas.*

_____

_____

_____

_____

_____

_____

_____

_____

_____

_____

LINKING IDEAS IN YOUR WRITING

To group types of information together, use **linking words.**
Some examples of linking words are: **another, for example, also, next,** and **because.** Revise the paragraph you wrote on the previous page adding linking words.

_____

_____

_____

_____

_____

_____

_____

_____

_____

_____

_____

_____

WRITING A NARRATIVE

The four pictures below tell a story. Use the pictures to help you tell the story of Alex using a carrot to ride the pig. Write on the back of the page if needed.

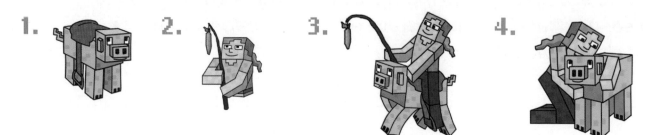

1.   2.   3.   4.

_____

_____

_____

_____

_____

_____

_____

_____

SEQUENCE OF EVENTS

In **expository writing,** *ideas, reasons, or steps are presented in a logical order. Place the sentences below in the correct order so the directions make sense.*

———————— **1.** Finally, enjoy watching your snow golem shoot snowballs at your enemies!

———————— **2.** Place the second snow block on top of the first one.

———————— **3.** If you want to make a snow golem, start with two snow blocks and a pumpkin in your inventory.

———————— **4.** After you stack the snow blocks, place the pump-kin on the top.

———————— **5.** Place one snow block down.

RECIPE FOR EXPOSITORY WRITING

Your health bar is getting low. It's time to make a potion of Healing. Describe the steps you would take to make or get this potion and restore your health. Use some of the words in the word box to show the order in which you would do things.

First	Then	Next	Secondly
After	Later	Finally	Lastly

_____

_____

_____

_____

_____

_____

_____

_____

_____

CHARACTER DEVELOPMENT

In writing, character development means the way a character in a story is revealed to the reader. It is always better to reveal a character's traits by what they say and do (showing) rather than describing those traits directly (telling). For example:

(telling)	*Alex was annoyed.*
(showing)	*Alex let out a big sigh and rolled her eyes.*

Pick one of the characters in the scene below. Imagine what that person is thinking, saying, and feeling. Then fill out the graphic organizer on the next page.

CHARACTER DEVELOPMENT

Read the instructions on the previous page and fill out the graphic organizer below. Remember, you can make up anything you want!

Name of your character: _____

Three character traits:

1. _____

2. _____

3. _____

What the character says	What the character does
How the character feels	What the character's body is doing

CHARACTER DEVELOPMENT

Using your graphic organizer from the previous page, write a short story about your character's day. Remember to show, not tell, the reader what your character is like.

_____

_____

_____

_____

_____

_____

_____

_____

_____

_____

_____

WRITING DIALOGUE

Let's continue the story you started on the previous page. Write at least five lines of dialogue to describe what happens next. Remember to use quotation marks and commas in the correct places.

_____

_____

_____

_____

_____

_____

_____

_____

_____

_____

_____

SIMILES

A **simile** is a figure of speech that directly compares two different things. A simile is usually in a phrase that begins with **as** or **like**.

Example: The airplane roared like a lion.
The pillow was as hard as a stone.

*Place an **S** next to the sentences that contain similes. Underline the simile in the sentence. The first one is done for you.*

_____S_____ **1.** The endermite was <u>as quiet as a mouse.</u>

_____ **2.** The lava was hot like the sun.

_____ **3.** The shovel was very sharp.

_____ **4.** The zombies were as green as spring grass.

_____ **5.** Steve slept like a baby.

_____ **6.** The sheep is dyed bright pink.

METAPHORS

A **metaphor** is a figure of speech that is used to make a comparison between two things that aren't alike but do have something in common.

Example: The classroom was a zoo.

*Place an **M** next to the sentences that contain metaphors. Underline the metaphor in the sentence. The first one is done for you.*

____M____ **1.** She is a <u>prickly cactus</u>.

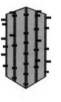

_____ **2.** He was a pig at dinner.

_____ **3.** My brother is a couch potato.

_____ **4.** The ghast was so angry that it screamed.

_____ **5.** That evoker is a real ogre.

_____ **6.** The sun was shining brightly.

ADAGES

An **adage** (also called a **proverb**) is an old, short saying that is generally accepted to have some truth to it.

Example: *Beauty is in the eye of the beholder.*
Meaning: *Everyone has a different idea of what is beautiful.*

Match the adage on the top with its meaning below. Write the letter on the line. The first one is done for you.

_____B_____ 1. Actions speak louder than words.

_____ 2. Don't cry over spilled milk.

_____ 3. The early bird catches the worm.

_____ 4. The grass is always greener on the other side of the fence.

_____ 5. Don't put all your eggs in one basket.

_____ 6. A picture is worth a thousand words.

A. Don't spend your time feeling bad about old mistakes.

B. What you do is more important than what you say.

C. The one who arrives first has the best chance for success.

D. An image conveys meaning better than a description does.

E. People are never satisfied with their own situation; they always think others have it better.

F. Don't put all your hopes on one thing that might not happen.

IDIOMS

An **idiom** is a phrase or an expression that means something different from its literal meaning.

Example: *It's raining cats and dogs.*
Meaning: *It's raining a lot.*

Match the idiom on the left to it's nonliteral meaning on the right. The first one is done for you.

1. On cloud nine

2. A piece of cake

3. A level playing field

4. Butterflies in my stomach

5. Back to square one

6. Hungry as a bear

7. A drop in the bucket

A. Famished, starving

B. A little bit of what is needed

C. Nervous

D. Very happy, elated

E. Equal, even

F. Starting all over again

G. Very easy

USING TECHNOLOGY

How much do you know about each Minecraft mob? With an adult's help, do some online research to learn more about one Minecraft mob. Use at least two websites. Take notes about what you learn in the space below.

_____

_____

_____

_____

_____

_____

_____

_____

_____

USING TECHNOLOGY

Using the notes you took on the previous page, write four new things you learned about the mob using the categories below.

1. Spawning

_____

2. Behavior

_____

3. Immunity

_____

4. Damage

_____

List the websites you used for your research.

1. _____

2. _____

3. _____

RUN-ON SENTENCES

A **run-on sentence** occurs when two or more complete sentences are joined without any form of punctuation.

Example: *I love to play Minecraft I would play every day if I had the time.*

To correct a run-on sentence, you have two choices:

1. Add a comma and the word *and* between the two sentences.

   Example: *I love to play Minecraft, and I would play every day if I had the time.*

2. Add a period at the end of the first sentence and start the next sentence with a capital letter.

   Example: *I love to play Minecraft. I would play every day if I had the time.*

Correct the run-on sentences below by breaking them into two sentences.

1. The creeper has block-shaped feet it is green.

   _____

2. Steve likes to tame wolves to keep as pets he puts red collars on them.

   _____

3. Alex fought the wither with all her strength her bow and arrow came in very handy.

   _____

RUN-ON SENTENCES

(Continued from previous page)

4. The player was very sneaky he stole everything out of my chest.

_____

5. Alex uses a pickaxe to mine for diamonds she will make a diamond sword when she is done.

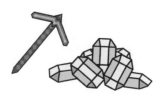

_____

6. Steve made eye contact with the Enderman the Enderman teleported toward him.

_____

7. Diamond swords are very useful they can destroy blazes, Endermen, and zombies.

_____

8. Building a house in Minecraft is fun you must add doors to keep out hostile mobs.

_____

DEAR FELLOW GAMER

Write a short letter to your best friend telling him/ her about the last thing you built in Minecraft and what you've learned about building in Minecraft. Your challenge: use as many of the sight words below as you can.

| built | certain | compare | complete | close | possible |

Dear _____,

_____

_____

_____

_____

_____

_____

Sincerely,

_____

DEAR MINECRAFT CREATOR

Write a short letter to the creator of Minecraft. Explain what you think is special about the game, ask questions, or make suggestions for improving the game. Your challenge: use as many of the sight words below as you can.

simple	since	someone	special	through

Dear Minecraft Creator,

_____

_____

_____

_____

_____

_____

_____

Sincerely,

_____

CAPITALIZATION AND PUNCTUATION RULES

Review the rules of capitalization and punctuation.

CAPITALIZATION RULES

Capitalize the first word of a sentence.

> Evoker casts many spells.

Capitalize proper nouns such as names of people, places, businesses, holidays, days, and months.

> The default player in Minecraft is named Steve.
> Snow golem's favorite holiday is Halloween.
> Halloween is on October 31.

Capitalize the first word in a quotation.

> Alex yelled, "Watch out!"

Capitalize the first and important words in a title of a book or song.

> Witch's favorite book is <u>The Big Book of Potions</u>.

PUNCTUATION RULES

End a sentence with a period, a question mark, or an exclamation point.

> Steve crafted a new sword.
> Have you seen Enderman?
> Creeper exploded!

Use a comma following each word in a series of three or more.

> Pig, chicken, and goat follow Alex around the farm.

Use a comma between the month and day and the year.

> Minecraft was released on May 17, 2009.

Use a comma to separate a quotation from the speaker.

> "Let's mine for diamonds," Steve said.

Use quotation marks to enclose a quote.

> "Yes," said Alex, "you ride the minecart to the mine."

Underline or italicize the title of a book or song.

> Creeper's favorite song is <u>You Blow My Mind</u>.

CAPITALIZATION AND PUNCTUATION PRACTICE

Review the capitalization and punctuation rules on page 270. Then rewrite each sentence, correcting the errors.

1. alex's cow and chicken had fun on the farm?

_____

2. librarian's favorite book is the atlas of minecraft biomes

_____

3. here is a poppy for you said iron golem to the villager

_____

4. Will snow golem melt on a hot sunny day.

_____

5. steve captured creeper on tuesday and put it in a trap

_____

WRITE YOUR OPINION

*Which of the following mobs is the most dangerous in Minecraft? Choose one and complete the paragraph below. First you will state your **point of view** and then give three **reasons**.*

The _____ is the most dangerous mob because

_____ .

Also, it _____ .

Finally, it _____ .

In conclusion, _____ is the most dangerous

of all the mobs above.

WRITE YOUR OPINION

Which mode of Minecraft is the best: Creative mode or Survival mode? Write your opinion below using any or all of the phrases in the phrase box.

| One way | Another way | In addition | In conclusion |

IN THE DESERT

Pretend you spawn (start in the game) in the Desert Biome. Describe how you would survive. Use details.

1. If I spawned in the desert, I would _____

_____ .

2. If I needed food, I would _____

_____ .

3. Finally, I would stay safe by _____

_____ .

IN THE DESERT

Use the details you wrote on the previous page to write a story about how you survived in the desert.

_____

_____

_____

_____

_____

_____

_____

_____

_____

_____

WRITE A STORY

Use the characters and setting to write a story.
Use the boxes to plan your story.

CHARACTERS

Polar Bear

Rabbit

Stray

SETTING

Snowy Tundra

BEGINNING	MIDDLE	ENDING
Who are the characters?	What happens to the characters along the way?	How does the character solve the problem?
What is the setting?		
What problem does the main character have?		

WRITE A STORY

Choose your characters and setting to write a story.
Use the boxes to plan your story.

BEGINNING	MIDDLE	ENDING
Who are the characters?	What happens to the characters along the way?	How does the character solve the problem?
What is the setting?		
What problem does the main character have?		

_____

_____

_____

_____

REVISING MY STORY

All good writers revise their writing. When you revise, you read your writing again to make it better. Use this checklist to revise one of the stories you wrote on pages 275, 277, or 278-279.

Answer the questions. If you can't answer yes, revise your writing until you can.

1. Does your story have a beginning that makes the reader want to read? _____

2. Does your story have good characters? _____

3. Does your story have an interesting setting? _____

4. Does your story have a problem that needs to be solved?

    _____

5. Does your story have an ending that solves the problem?

    _____

6. Did you add interesting details? _____

7. Does your story make sense? _____

8. Is your story at least three paragraphs long? _____

Rewrite your story on the computer or on another sheet of paper.

EDITING MY STORY

After you have revised your story, it's time to edit. When you edit, you make sure that your story is easy to read. Use this checklist to edit the story you revised on the previous page.

- [ ] I have reread my story, and it makes sense.

- [ ] Every sentence has a capital letter.

- [ ] Every paragraph is indented.

- [ ] All proper nouns begin with a capital letter.

- [ ] The first and important words in the title of my story have capital letters.

- [ ] Every sentence ends with the correct punctuation.

- [ ] Quotation marks are used correctly.

- [ ] All of the words are spelled correctly.

- [ ] My subjects and verbs go together.

Read your story to a friend or family member.

MINECRAFT HAIKU

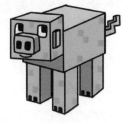

A haiku is a three-line poem that uses syllable patterns. Read the haiku poem. Then write your own about one of your favorite mobs.

HAIKU SYLLABLE PATTERN

five syllables	passive pig is pink
seven syllables	dropping porkchops when they die
five syllables	tamed with a carrot

Write Your Own

_____

_____

_____

TANKA POEM

A tanka poem is like a haiku poem, but with two more lines. Read the tanka poem. Then write your own about one of your favorite mobs.

five syllables	hostile flying blaze
seven syllables	lives in the nether fortress
five syllables	sinking down slowly
seven syllables	avoids water and lava
seven syllables	shoots trios of fireballs

Write Your Own

_____

_____

_____

_____

_____

DIAMOND POEM

Diamond poems compare two opposites. Read the diamond poem below. Write your own diamond poem about the transformation of a mob.

Pig
pink, passive
wandering, eating, oinking
pet, lightning, transformation, zombie
destroying, spawning, pathfinding
undead, neutral
Zombie Pigman

Name a mob	_____
Write two adjectives describing the mob	_____ , _____
Write three "ing" words describing the mob.	_____ , _____ , _____
Write four nouns. The first two nouns relate to the mob and the second two nouns relate to the transformed mob.	_____ , _____ , _____ , _____
Write three "ing" words describing the transformed mob.	_____ , _____ , _____
Write two adjectives describing the transformed mob.	_____ , _____
Name a transformed mob.	_____

CINQUAINS

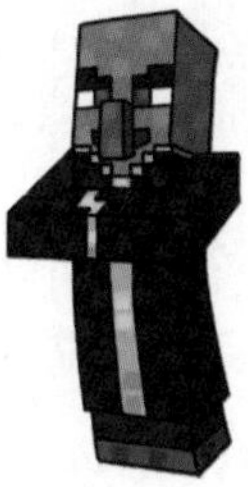

A cinquain is a five-line poem similar to the diamond poem. Read the cinquain and notice its pattern. Then write your own.

Line 1: one noun	evoker
Line 2: two adjectives describing the noun	magical, hostile
Line 3: three "ing" verbs describing the noun	spell-casting, raiding, vexing
Line 4: a four-word phrase describing the noun	drops totem of undying
Line 5: a synonym for the noun	villager

Write Your Own

_____

_____

_____

_____

MINECRAFT COMIC STRIPS

Write what the players and mobs might be saying to each other. Add talk bubbles. Make it funny. Think of riddles and jokes you know. The first one is done for you.

Do you know what Alex said to pig when it became irritated?

Keep calm and carrot on.

MORE MINECRAFT COMIC STRIPS

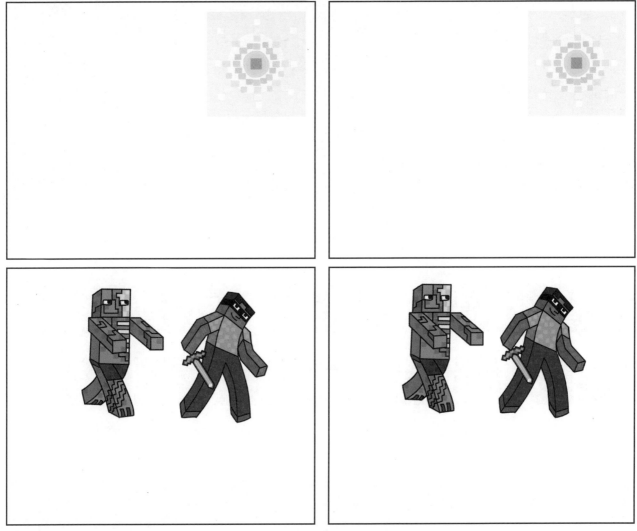

Draw your own!

PUZZLES AND GAMES
FOR MINECRAFTERS

HEAR THIS!

Write the name of each Minecraft Earth item on the spaces. Solve the riddle by replacing each number pair in the code with a letter in one of the icon names. For instance, 1-4 means the fourth letter in the first word below.

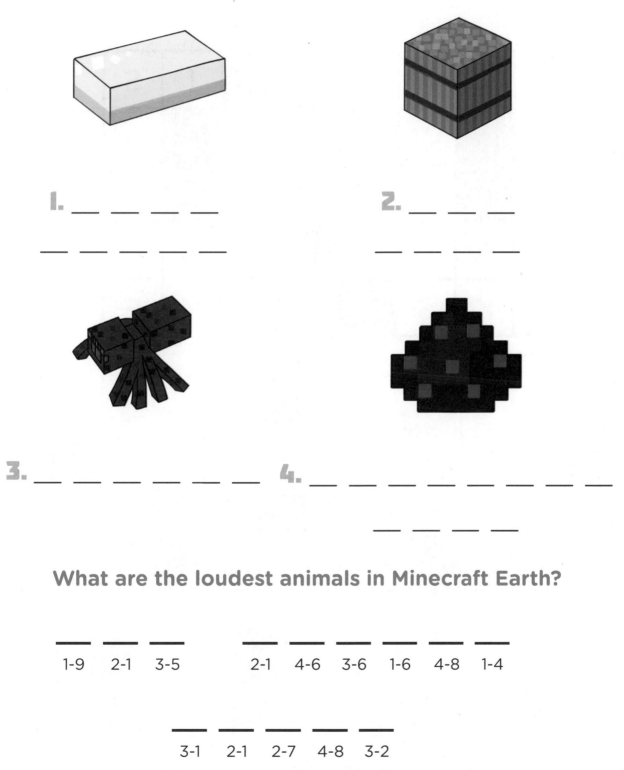

1. _ _ _ _ _

_ _ _ _ _

2. _ _ _

_ _ _ _

3. _ _ _ _ _ _

4. _ _ _ _ _ _ _ _

_ _ _ _

What are the loudest animals in Minecraft Earth?

— — —   — — — — — —
1-9 2-1 3-5   2-1 4-6 3-6 1-6 4-8 1-4

— — — — —
3-1 2-1 2-7 4-8 3-2

TEAM BUILDING

Build the word wall on this buildplate by placing the 2x2 letter blocks in their proper places. If you place them correctly, you'll reveal the trick to Minecraft Earth team building. **Heads up:** Words are separated by black squares and wrap from one line to the next.

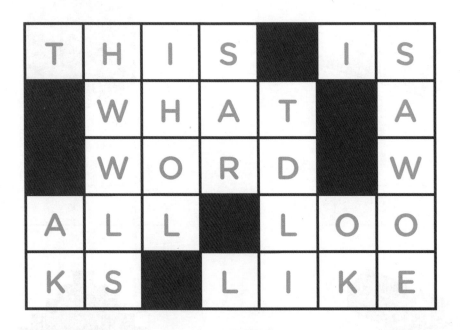

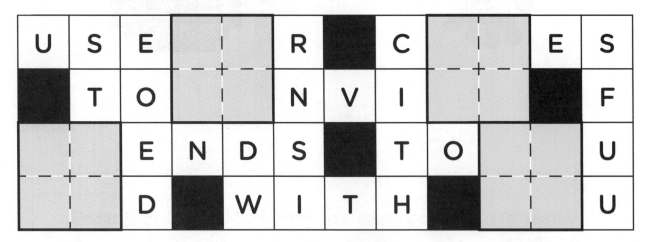

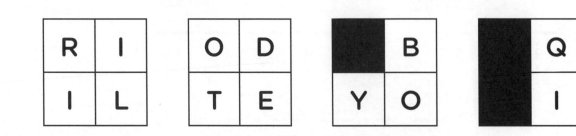

DANCE PARTY DISASTERS

Crack the code. Write the name of each icon on the spaces provided. Replace each number pair in the code with a letter in one of the icon names. For instance, 2-4 means the fourth letter in word #2 below.

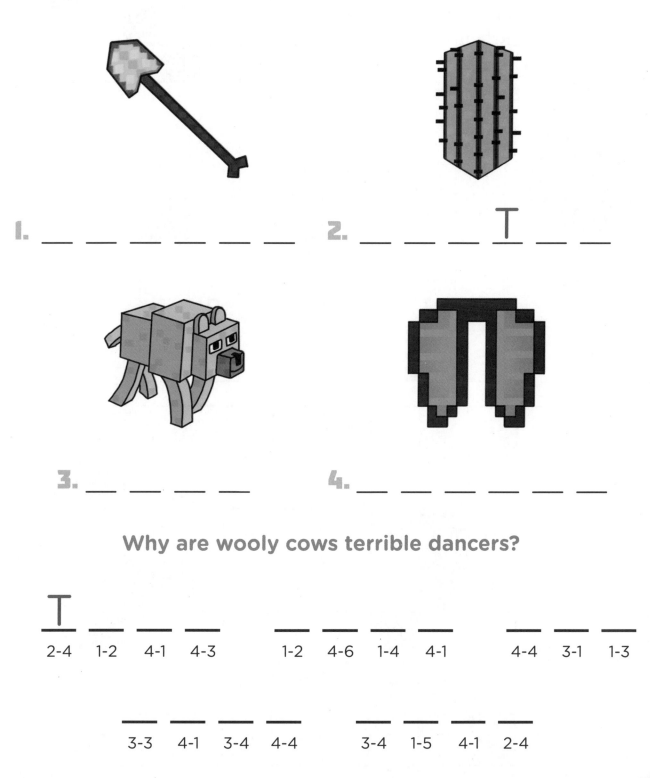

1. __ __ __ __ __ __ __

2. __ __ __ T __ __ __

3. __ __ __ __ __

4. __ __ __ __ __ __ __

Why are wooly cows terrible dancers?

T __ __ __ __ __ __ __ __ __ __ __ __
2-4 1-2 4-1 4-3   1-2 4-6 1-4 4-1   4-4 3-1 1-3

__ __ __ __ __ __ __ __
3-3 4-1 3-4 4-4   3-4 1-5 4-1 2-4

DISASTER WARNING

Build the word wall on this buildplate by placing the 2x2 letter blocks in their proper places. If you place them correctly, you'll reveal a tip that might help prevent a disaster. **Heads up:** Words are separated by black squares and wrap from one line to the next.

T	H	I	S		I		S
	W	H	A	T			A
	W	O	R	D			W
A	L	L			L	O	O
K	S			L	I	K	E

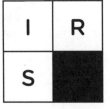

A	N
E	R

I	O
E	

I	R
S	

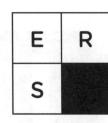

E	R
S	

I	N
A	R

P	R
T	E

F			E		S				E	A
D			F	A	S				R	
I	N		M			E	C	R	A	
F	T		E			T	H			T
H				O	T	H				
V			S			N				O
F		T	H			G	A	M	E	

PUNNY BUSINESS

Write the name of each icon on the spaces. Replace each number pair in the code with a letter in one of the icon names to solve the riddle. For instance, 1-4 means the fourth letter in the first word below.

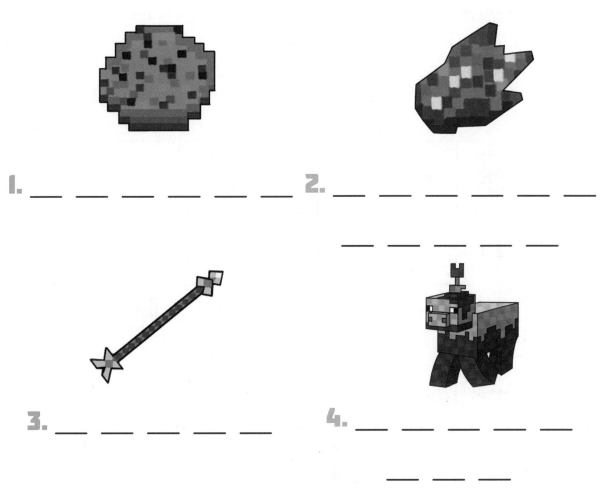

1. __ __ __ __ __ __ __

2. __ __ __ __ __ __ __

   __ __ __ __

3. __ __ __ __ __

4. __ __ __ __ __

   __ __ __ __

**What did the cobblestone block say
to the Minecraft Earth player?**

'

__ __ __ __   __ __ __ __   __ __
4-4 1-3 2-6 2-3   2-4 3-1 1-4 2-9   4-1 1-6

__ __ __   __ __ __ __ __ __ __
2-7 3-4 3-2   4-8 3-3 3-1 2-6 1-5 2-4 2-5

STUCK!

Can you find your way out of this desert maze without getting stuck? (On a cactus, that is.) Move in the direction an arrow points until you come to a new sign. If there are two arrows in a box, you can choose to go either direction. Can you go find the path that leads from START to FINISH and avoids the cacti?

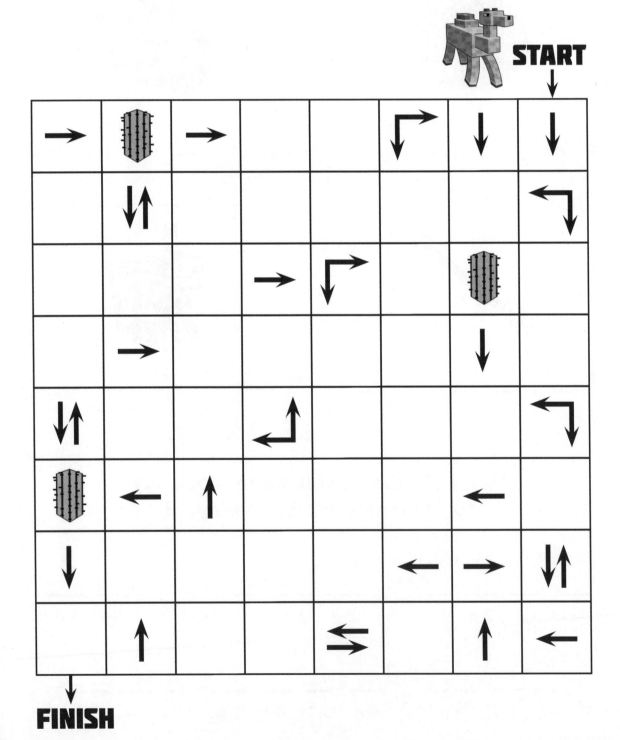

START

FINISH

A RARE DROP

Can you find the word MOOBLOOM in the letters below to get it to drop into your inventory? It appears only once in a horizontal, vertical, or diagonal line.

M M O O B L O M O O O

O O M L O B O O M M B

M M O O O B L O O M M

B O L M O M L O B O

M M O O L B M L L O

B O L L O O O B O L

L B B O B O O O O B

O M M L M O M B M O

O M O O L B O M O M

M O O L O B O M M L

TIP FOR TAPS

Here's a tip we all can use: To find out what it is, build the word wall on this buildplate by placing the 2x2 letter blocks in their proper places. If you place them correctly, you'll reveal a tip that unlocks more Minecraft Earth fun. **Heads up:** Words are separated by black squares and wrap from one line to the next.

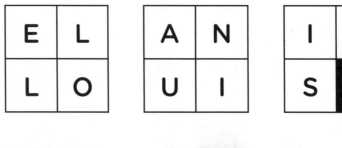

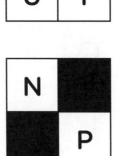

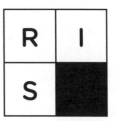

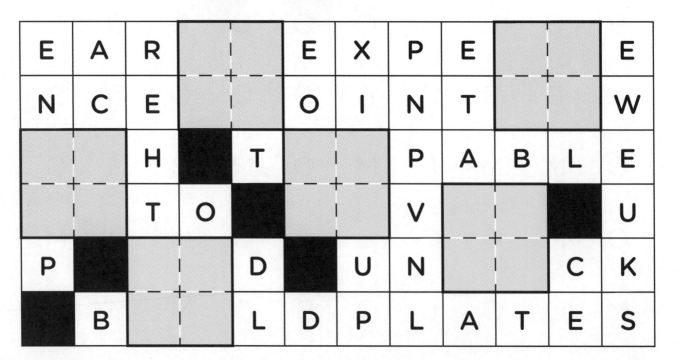

296

WORD TO THE WISE

Crack the code for a handy piece of advice about buildplates in Minecraft Earth. Write the name of each icon on the spaces. Replace each number pair in the code with a letter in one of the icon names. For instance, 1-4 is the fourth letter in the first word below.

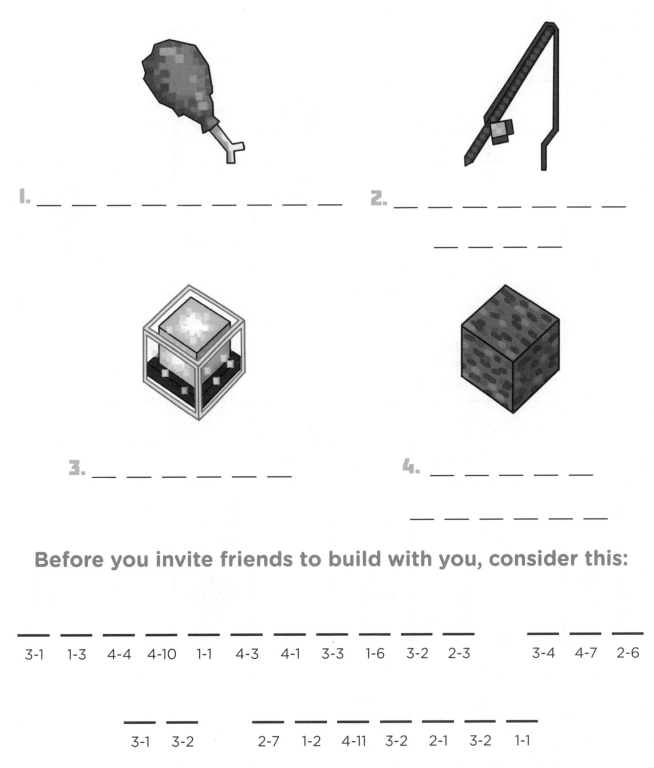

1. __ __ __ __ __ __ __ __ __ __

2. __ __ __ __ __ __ __
   __ __ __ __

3. __ __ __ __ __ __

4. __ __ __ __ __
   __ __ __ __ __ __

Before you invite friends to build with you, consider this:

__ __ __ __ __ __ __ __ __ __ __ __ __ __
3-1 1-3 4-4 4-10 1-1 4-3 4-1 3-3 1-6 3-2 2-3   3-4 4-7 2-6

__ __ __ __ __ __ __ __ __
3-1 3-2   2-7 1-2 4-11 3-2 2-1 3-2 1-1

KABOOM!

Can you find your way through this dangerous maze without running into TNT? Move in the direction an arrow points until you come to a new sign. If there are two arrows in a box, you can choose to go either direction.

START　　　　　　　　　　　　　　　　**FINISH**

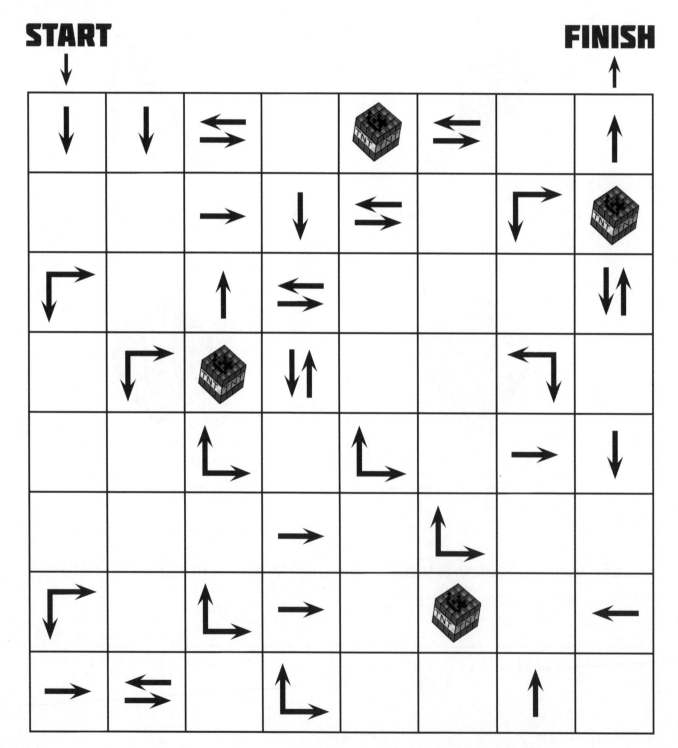

ATTENTION, EARTH THINGS

Can you find all the Minecraft Earth things in the word search? They might be forward, backward, up, down, or diagonal. Write unused letters on the blank spaces, in order from top to bottom and left to right to discover something useful to know.

Hint: Circle individual letters instead of whole words to better isolate remaining letters. We've found one to get you started.

```
I  W  O  O  L  Y  C  O  W  M  F
Y  A  M  A  L  L  Y  L  L  O  J
M  O  E  U  S  H  E  M  A  O  B
R  O  A  M  M  O  U  O  T  R  E
B  L  O  O  F  D  O  A  M  H  A
B  U  I  L  D  O  P  Y  O  S  C
U  W  I  Y  B  P  B  L  L  K  O
G  E  P  T  A  O  A  O  B  C  N
T  I  B  B  A  R  O  B  M  U  J
G  U  L  T  T  E  R  M  C  L  U
T  E  K  C  U  B  D  U  M  C  P
```

BEACON
BUILD
CLUCKSHROOM
JOLLY LLAMA
JUMBO RABBIT
MOB OF ME
MOOBLOOM
MUD BUCKET
MUDDY PIG
TAPPABLE
~~WOOLY COW~~

__ ___ _____ _

_____ , ____ ____

____ _ _____ .

TAP AND GO

You've located a tappable pink sheep, but two skeletons roam nearby. Make your way to the sheep without coming into contact with the skeletons or their sharp arrows.

START **FINISH**

A SLIPPERY SLOPE

Two Minecraft Earth resources are best kept separate. To find out what they are, write the name of each icon on the spaces. Replace each number pair in the code with a letter in one of the icon names. For instance, 1-4 is the fourth letter in the first word below.

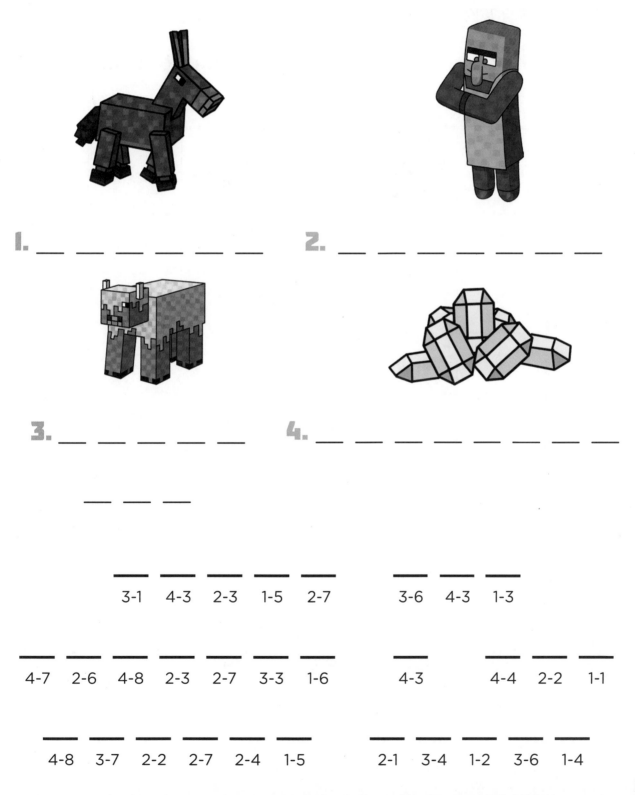

1. __ __ __ __ __ __

2. __ __ __ __ __ __ __

3. __ __ __ __ __ __

__ __ __ __

4. __ __ __ __ __ __ __

__ __ __ __ __
3-1 4-3 2-3 1-5 2-7   3-6 4-3 1-3

__ __ __ __ __ __ __   __   __ __ __
4-7 2-6 4-8 2-3 2-7 3-3 1-6   4-3   4-4 2-2 1-1

__ __ __ __ __ __   __ __ __ __ __
4-8 3-7 2-2 2-7 2-4 1-5   2-1 3-4 1-2 3-6 1-4

HERE, BOY

Use the picture-number combination under each missing letter space to find the correct letter on the grid. The correct letter is the one where the picture and number intersect. If you fill in the spaces correctly, you'll discover the answer to the riddle.

Why are illusioners like well-trained dogs?

1	G	P	A	S
2	O	F	H	C
3	D	I	E	Z
4	L	M	N	R

They come on

___ 2 ___ 2 ___ 4 ___ 4 ___ 1 ___ 4 ___ 3

A SMASHING SUCCESS

Use the picture-number combination under each blank space to find the correct letter on the grid. The correct letter is the one where the picture and number intersect. If you fill in the spaces correctly, you'll discover a fun tip that can help you be a smashing success!

	🪓	🦴	🐺	🍗
1	T	K	N	A
2	I	U	H	B
3	G	E	R	M
4	C	W	L	O

A player in a minecart on a rail can ride

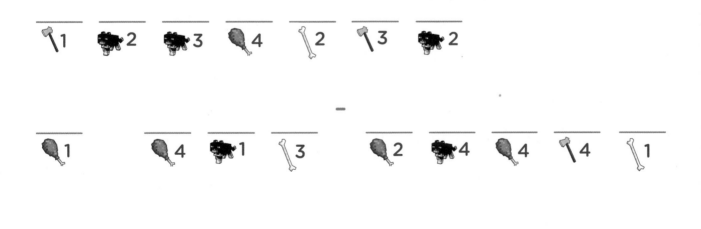

303

ENDLESS ENCHANTMENTS

The first and second scales are balanced. How many ● do you need to balance the third scale? Draw them or write the number on the scale. If you balance the scale correctly, you will be able to enchant every item in your inventory!

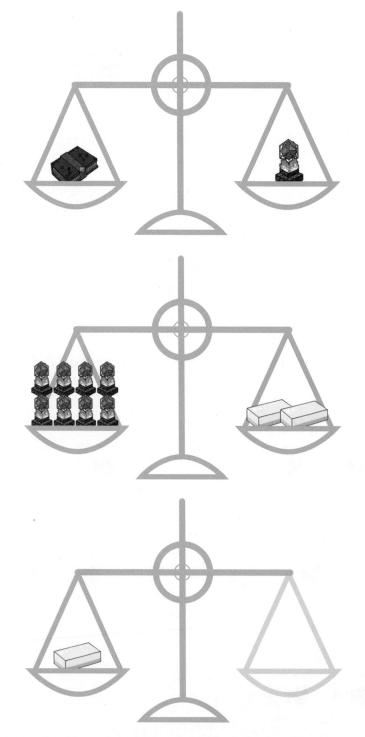

FIRE POWER

Move from box to box as you count by threes. Write the letter from each box where you land on the spaces, in order from left to right. Begin with the number 3 and continue until all the spaces are filled. If you count, hop, and copy letters correctly, you'll fill in the blank below.

A crossbow loaded with fireworks will

damage _____, even at long range.

30 M 18	15 R 25	21 E 19
23 U 13	12 E ③	6 N 24
28 C 16	9 D 27	8 P 22

E __ __ __ __ __ __ __

MORE MAGIC NUMBERS

If you fail to solve this puzzle, your ship is sunk!

The numbers at the end of the rows and columns are linked to the images in the grid. What number goes in the circle? This is the magic number for this puzzle.

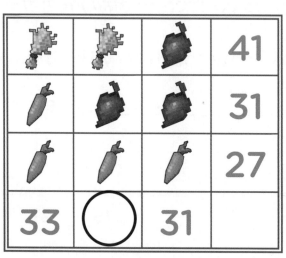

Circle the problems below that have the magic number as their answer. Unscramble those letters to spell the answer to the joke.

Why did the nitwit sink the boat with too much iron, gold, and redstone?

19	5	4	47	57	49
+16	x7	x8	-12	-22	- 7

E	N	J	O	S	G
28	32	41	6	7	21
+7	+ 3	- 6	x2	x5	+14

D	A	E	K	I	R

Because he heard the captain say,

" _____ "

___ ___ ___ ___   ___ ___ ___ ___ ___ .

SPUH-LASH

Splash texts are the yellow lines of text on the title screen. They might be inside jokes, bits of advice, or nonsense.

Use the picture-number combination under each missing letter space to find the correct letter on the grid. The correct letter is the one where the picture and number intersect. If you fill in the spaces correctly, you'll discover splash text that's also a useful piece of Minecraft advice.

	🪓	⛏️	🔨	🪏
1	G	V	E	U
2	A	P	O	D
3	R	I	H	W
4	Z	C	N	T

___ ___ ___ ___ ___
4   1   1   1   3

___ ___ ___
2   3   1

___ ___ ___ ___
2   2   3   4

SLOW GOING

Cobwebs are great for slowing down mobs and arrows, but they have another clever use, too.

Use the picture-number combination under each blank letter space to find the correct letter on the grid. The correct letter is the one where the picture and number intersect. If you fill in the spaces correctly, you'll discover another fun use for cobwebs.

Use cobwebs to create delays in _____.

	🍪	💎	🥚	🌹
1	D	A	T	N
2	U	B	K	R
3	O	C	S	G
4	W	E	L	I

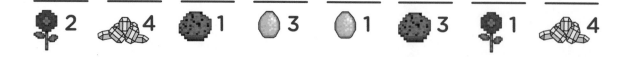

308

LOOKING UP

Have you ever gotten lost in Minecraft? Use the picture-number combination under each blank letter space to find the correct letter on the grid. The correct letter is the one where the picture and number intersect. If you fill in the spaces correctly, you'll discover a unique method for finding your way in Minecraft.

1	O	A	T	H
2	Y	P	E	M
3	B	K	W	R
4	L	V	X	S

Watch the sun, moon, stars, and clouds, because they

___ 1 ___ 4 ___ 3 ___ 1 ___ 2 ___ 4

___ 2 ___ 1 ___ 4 ___ 2   ___ 3 ___ 2 ___ 4 ___ 1

THE POINT IS. . . SHARP!

The first and second scales are balanced. How many  do you need to balance the third scale? Draw them or write the number on the scale before the cactus rolls and you feel its spikes. Ouch!

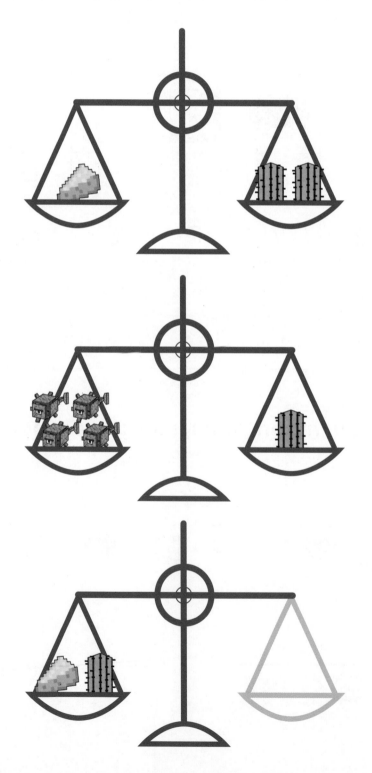

ASK AND RECEIVE

Hop from box to box counting by sevens. Write the letter from each box where you land on the spaces, in order from left to right, until all spaces are filled.

If you count, hop, and copy letters correctly, you'll reveal the decorative item that was added at the suggestion of a Minecraft fan like you.

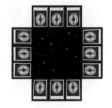

31	35	62	56
I	F	U	M
⑦	46	45	28
60	70	22	38
R	S	T	Y
42	25	14	29
50	24	63	43
D	Q	E	A
13	32	21	49

I __ __ __ __

__ __ __ __ __

YOUR FATE, IN THE BALANCE

As long as the scales are balanced, you are safe. As soon as one tips, even the slightest bit, you're a goner. The first and second scales are balanced. How many 👾 do you need to balance the third scale? Draw them or write the number on the scale before the lava or the strays destroy you!

A NETHER JOKE

Beginning with the number 14, move from box to box by adding 3 each time you move. Write the letter from each box where you land on the spaces, in order from left to right, until all spaces are filled. If you count, hop, and copy letters correctly, you'll reveal the punchline to this joke:

Did you hear about the Minecraft player who went to sleep in the Nether?

20 **C** 11	50 **E** 29	23 **A** 38	53 **N** 46
35 **O** 59	(14) **H** 55	22 **A** 33	32 **T** 51
26 **M** 37	47 **D** 56	17 **E** 44	8 **B** 41

H __ __   __ __ __ __ __ __   __ __ __

__ __ __ __ __ __ __ !

A SLIMING SCALE

The first and second scales are balanced. How many 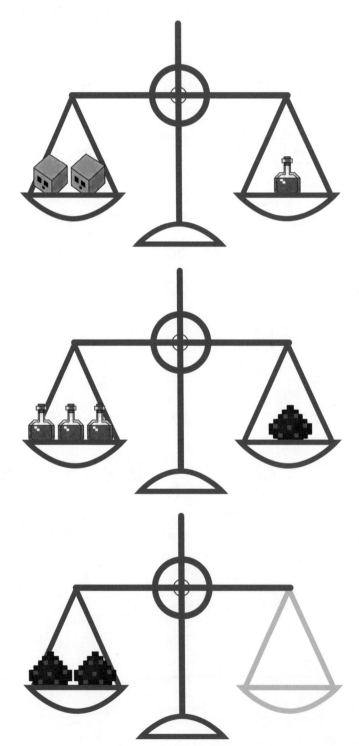 *do you need to balance the third scale? Draw them or write the number on the scale. If you balance the scale correctly, you get to keep the redstone.*

MINING SHORTCUT

This shortcut can save you tons of time. Beginning with the number 22, move from box to box by adding 4 each time you move. Write the letter from each box where you land on the spaces, in order from left to right, until all spaces are filled. If you count, hop, and copy letters correctly, you'll reveal a time-saving mining technique.

30 86		78 82	
N	S	H	E
84	(22) 56	54	
25 58	42	34	
I	L	R	D
72	32	70	40
66	92	52	88
O	G	Y	T
90	38	60	62
50 80		46 74	
V	F	A	C
94	76	26	64

Mine S __ __ __ and __ __ __ __ __ __

with __ __ __ __ __ __ __ .

CREEPER'S WORD LADDER

Solve this word ladder using the clues provided. Start with the word at the bottom and move your way up the ladder.

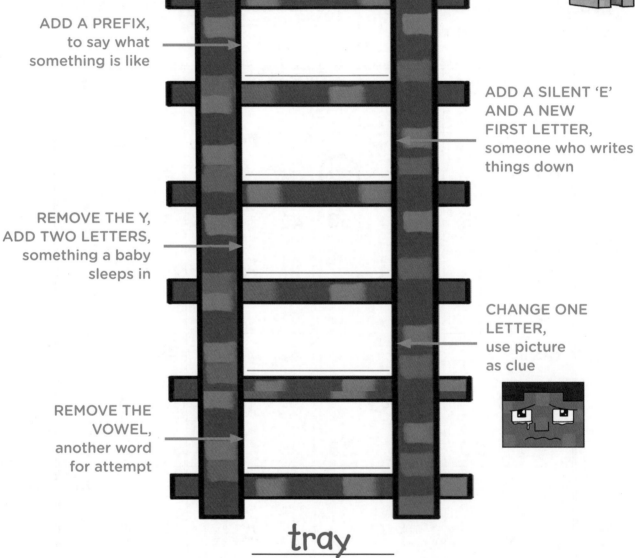

ADD A PREFIX, to say what something is like

ADD A SILENT 'E' AND A NEW FIRST LETTER, someone who writes things down

REMOVE THE Y, ADD TWO LETTERS, something a baby sleeps in

CHANGE ONE LETTER, use picture as clue

REMOVE THE VOWEL, another word for attempt

tray

ALEX'S WORD LADDER

Solve this word ladder using the clues provided. Start with the word at the bottom and move your way up the ladder.

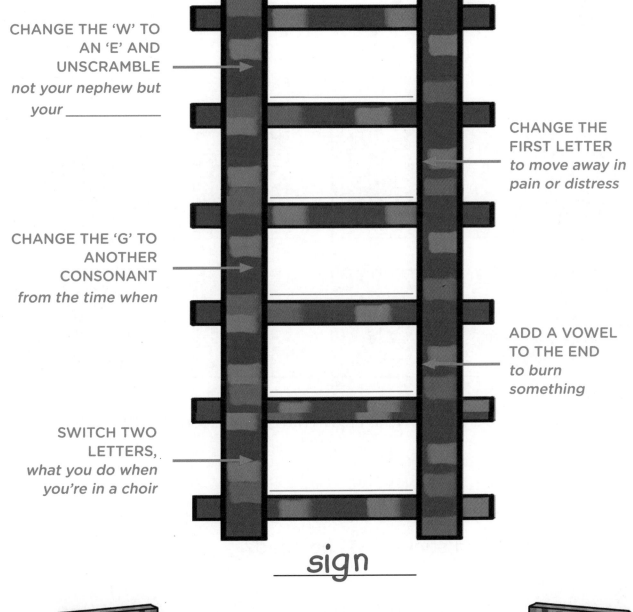

CHANGE THE 'W' TO AN 'E' AND UNSCRAMBLE
not your nephew but your _____

CHANGE THE FIRST LETTER
to move away in pain or distress

CHANGE THE 'G' TO ANOTHER CONSONANT
from the time when

ADD A VOWEL TO THE END
to burn something

SWITCH TWO LETTERS,
what you do when you're in a choir

sign

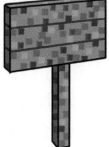

CRAFT RECIPES

Look at the crafting recipes. Answer the questions.

| diamond | diamond block | stick | diamond axe | diamond shovel | diamond sword |

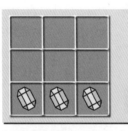   

1. Steve has 63 diamonds. How many diamond blocks can he craft? _____

2. Steve wants to craft 8 diamond swords. How many diamonds and sticks does he need? _____

3. Steve has 26 diamonds. How many diamond axes can he craft? _____

4. Steve wants to craft 5 diamond axes, 4 diamond shovels, and 6 diamond swords. How many diamonds and sticks will he need? _____

CRAFTING DIAMOND ARMOR

Look at the crafting recipes. Answer the questions.

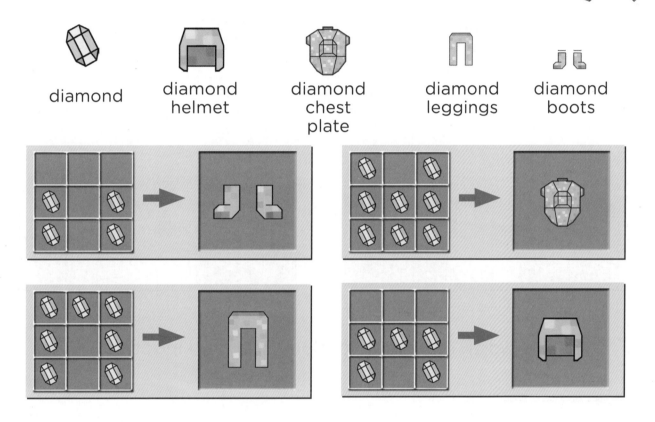

diamond   diamond helmet   diamond chest plate   diamond leggings   diamond boots

1. Steve is crafting 8 diamond suits of armor. Write multiplication problems to show how many diamonds he will need to craft the helmets, chest plates, leggings, and boots he will need.

2. Steve has 40 diamonds. Write division problems to show how many of each armor item he could craft.

EUREKA!

Look at the value of gold. Answer the questions.

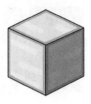

gold
block

gold
ingot

gold
nugget

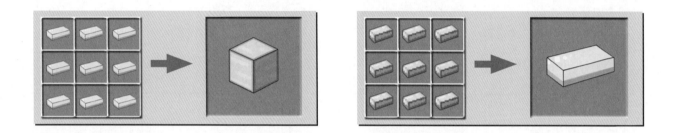

1. Which is worth more: a gold block or a gold ingot?

_____

2. Which is worth more: a gold nugget or a gold ingot?

_____

3. Alex has 5 gold blocks. How many gold ingots can she craft?

_____

4. Alex wants to craft 2 gold blocks. How many gold nuggets

will she need? _____

ALL THAT GLITTERS

*Look at the crafting tables. Then answer the
questions and help Alex craft some gold tools.*

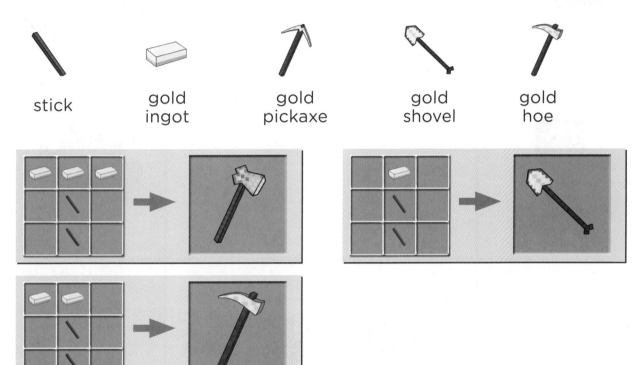

stick   gold   gold   gold   gold
               ingot   pickaxe   shovel   hoe

1. Alex has 3 gold ingots and 2 sticks. What tool can she craft?

_____

2. Alex wants to craft 2 gold pickaxes, 3 gold shovels, and 1
gold hoe. How many gold ingots and sticks will she need?

_____

3. Alex has 6 gold ingots and 6 sticks. She could craft 1 gold
pickaxe, 1 gold shovel, and 1 gold hoe. Write 2 other
combinations of tools she could craft.

_____

MINECRAFT SUDOKU 1

Draw an ocean mob in each square. The trick is to have only one of each ocean mob in each 4 x 4 box, each column, each row, and diagonally.

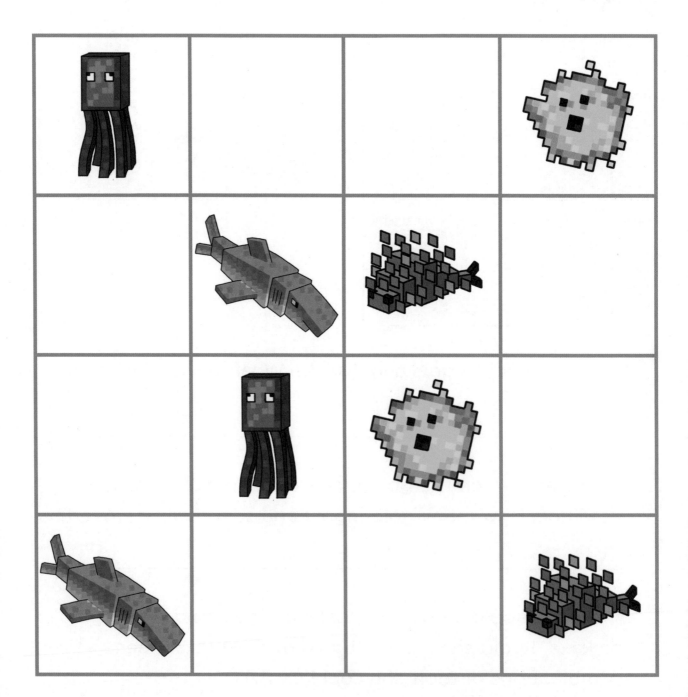

MINECRAFT SUDOKU 2

Draw one piece of diamond gear in each square.
The trick is to have only one of each piece of diamond
gear in each 4 x 4 box, each column, each row, and diagonally.

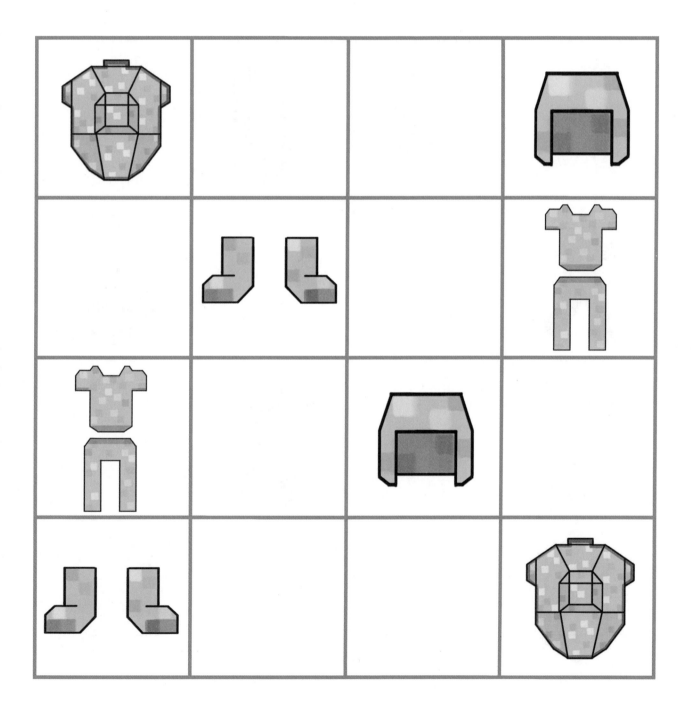

MINECRAFT SUDOKU 3

Draw a desert mob in each square. The trick is to have only one of each desert mob in each 4 x 4 box, each column, each row, and diagonally.

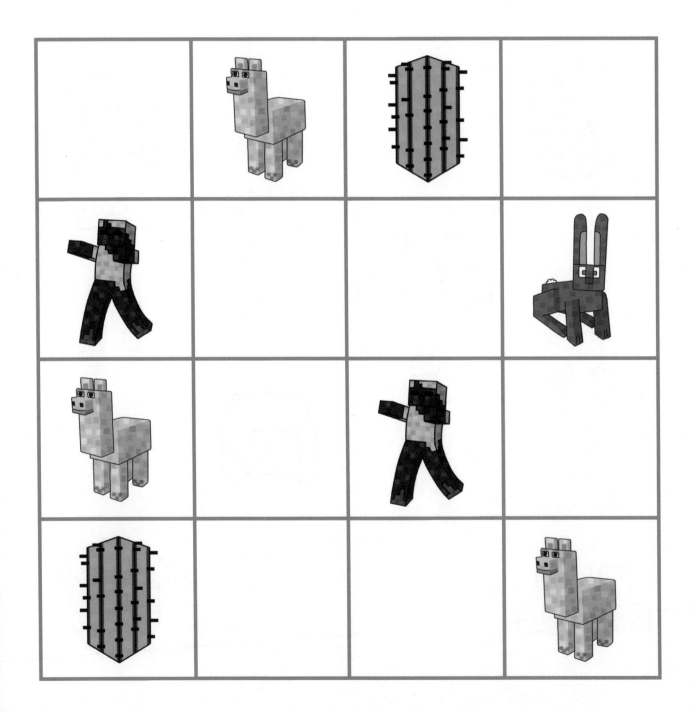

MINECRAFT SUDOKU 4

Draw a potion in each square. The trick is to have only one of each potion in each 4 x 4 box, each column, each row, and diagonally.

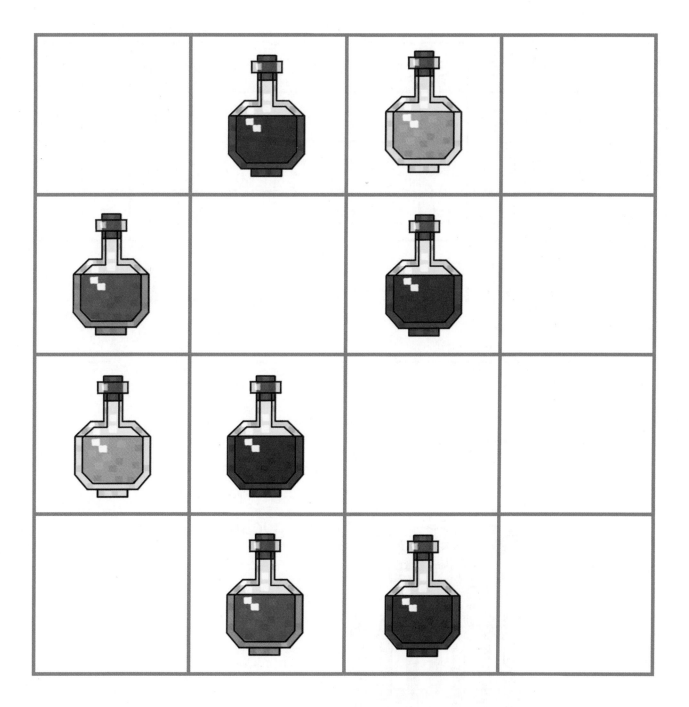

CRACK THE CODE 1

Use the decoder to solve the riddle.

DECODER												
A	B	C	D	E	F	G	H	I	J	K	L	M
6	22	12	25	20	8	1	23	14	18	10	2	19
N	O	P	Q	R	S	T	U	V	W	X	Y	Z
26	7	3	24	13	21	16	4	15	9	17	5	11

Why is pig the least popular mob on the farm?

$\frac{}{22}$ $\frac{}{20}$ $\frac{}{12}$ $\frac{}{6}$ $\frac{}{4}$ $\frac{}{21}$ $\frac{}{20}$ $\frac{}{14}$ $\frac{}{16}$ $\frac{}{14}$ $\frac{}{21}$ $\frac{}{6}$

$\frac{}{22}$ $\frac{}{7}$ $\frac{}{6}$ $\frac{}{13}$

Excuse me.
I take a fence to
that question!

CRACK THE CODE 2

Use the decoder to solve the riddles.

DECODER												
A	B	C	D	E	F	G	H	I	J	K	L	M
6	22	12	25	20	8	1	23	14	18	10	2	19
N	O	P	Q	R	S	T	U	V	W	X	Y	Z
26	7	3	24	13	21	16	4	15	9	17	5	11

1. Where did the butcher dance?

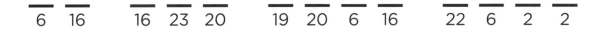

— —   — — —   — — — —   — — — —
6 16   16 23 20   19 20 6 16   22 6 2 2

2. What kind of music does rabbit like best?

— — —   — — —
23 14 3   23 7 3

Would you like to dance?

I'd be hoppy to!

327

CRACK THE CODE 3

Use the decoder to solve the riddles.

DECODER												
A	B	C	D	E	F	G	H	I	J	K	L	M
6	22	12	25	20	8	1	23	14	18	10	2	19
N	O	P	Q	R	S	T	U	V	W	X	Y	Z
26	7	3	24	13	21	16	4	15	9	17	5	11

1. **What room in the house do undead mobs avoid?**

$\overline{16}\ \overline{23}\ \overline{20}\quad \overline{2}\ \overline{14}\ \overline{15}\ \overline{14}\ \overline{26}\ \overline{1}\quad \overline{13}\ \overline{7}\ \overline{7}\ \overline{19}$

2. **What kind of humor do undead mobs like best?**

$\overline{25}\ \overline{20}\ \overline{6}\ \overline{25}\quad \overline{3}\ \overline{6}\ \overline{26}$

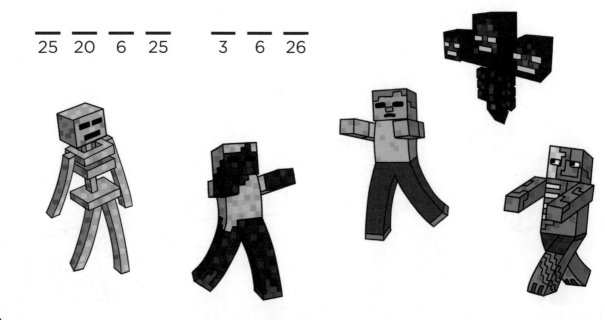

CRACK THE CODE 4

Use the decoder to solve the riddles.

DECODER

A	B	C	D	E	F	G	H	I	J	K	L	M
6	22	12	25	20	8	1	23	14	18	10	2	19

N	O	P	Q	R	S	T	U	V	W	X	Y	Z
26	7	3	24	13	21	16	4	15	9	17	5	11

1. **Why did skeleton cross the road?**

$\overline{}_{26}\ \overline{}_{7}\ \overline{}_{22}\ \overline{}_{7}\ \overline{}_{25}\ \overline{}_{5}\quad \overline{}_{10}\ \overline{}_{26}\ \overline{}_{7}\ \overline{}_{9}\ \overline{}_{21}$

2. **What did skeleton order at the restaurant?**

$\overline{}_{21}\ \overline{}_{3}\ \overline{}_{6}\ \overline{}_{13}\ \overline{}_{20}\quad \overline{}_{13}\ \overline{}_{14}\ \overline{}_{22}\ \overline{}_{21}$

FARM RIDDLES

Use the picture-number combination to solve the riddle. The correct letter is the one where the picture and the number come together.

	🐐	🐄	🐔	🐖	🐴
1	F	B	E	C	D
2	R	T	A	K	Y
3	H	L	O	S	N
4	M	W	U	I	G

1. Why did the farmer plant a new crop?

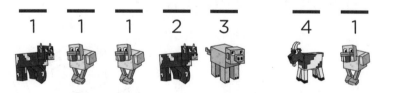

1	1	1	2	3	4	1

2. How do chickens bake a cake?

1	2	3	4	3	1	2	2	2	1	3

MORE FARM RIDDLES

3. **What do you get if you cross a chicken and a cow?**

| 2 | 3 | 3 | 3 | 2 | | 1 | 1 | 1 | 1 |

4. **What do you call it when it rains chickens?**

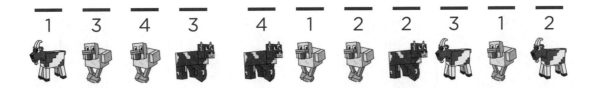

| 1 | 3 | 4 | 3 | | 4 | 1 | 2 | 2 | 3 | 1 | 2 |

5. **Why can't you shock a cow?**

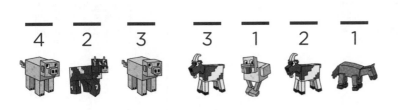

| 4 | 2 | 3 | | 3 | 1 | 2 | 1 |

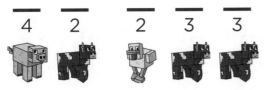

| 4 | 2 | | 2 | 3 | 3 |

6. **What type of horse goes out only at night?**

| 2 | | 3 | 4 | 4 | 3 | 2 | 4 | 2 | 2 | 1 |

WHAT COMES NEXT?

Find the pattern. Circle the square or group of squares that comes next.

1.

2.

3.

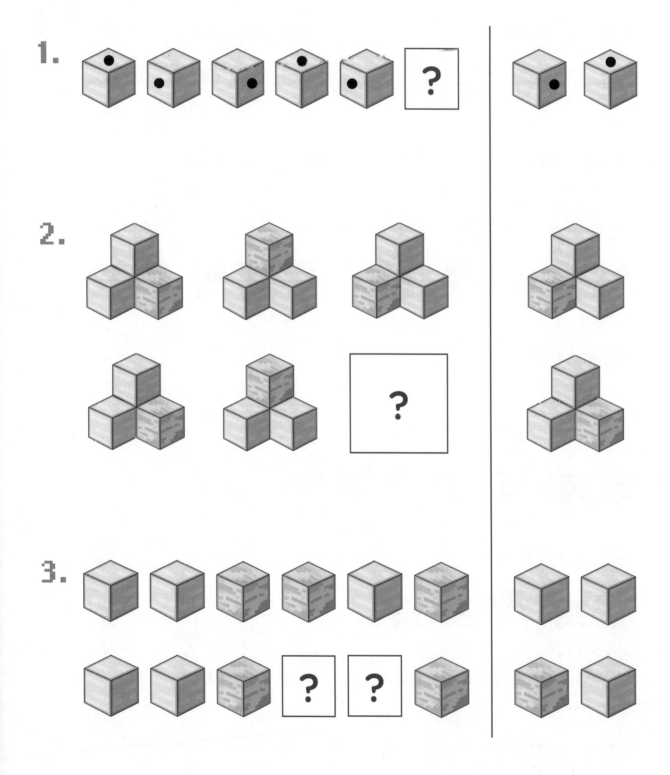

MOB MASKS

Copy the pattern to create these mob masks.

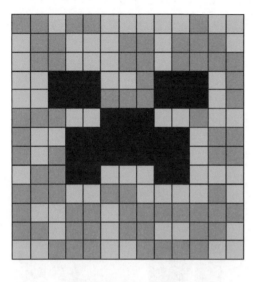

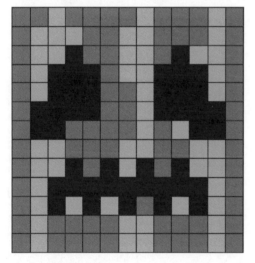

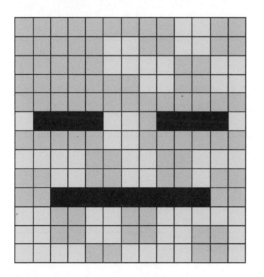

COLLECTING COWS

Some of Steve's cows have wandered away from the herd and are hiding in unusual places. Use the clues to find out where Steve's cows are hiding. Note that only one cow can be in each place.

Hint: Put an X in the box when you know that a cow was not found in a place. Put an O in the box when you know where a cow was found.

- Mooshroom is not in the mushroom field.
- Moobloom and cow are not in the barn.
- Sunset cow was eating flowers in the garden.
- Cow avoids the mushroom field.

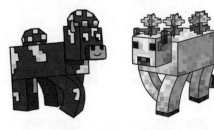

	In the Garden	In the Tall Grass	In the Mushroom Field	In the Barn
COW				
MOOSHROOM				
MOOBLOOM				
SUNSET COW				

LOGIC IN THE END

Danger lurks everywhere in the End. Beware the dangerous mobs. Use the clues to determine where the mobs might be hiding. Note that only one mob can be in each place.

Hint: Put an X in the box when you know that a mob was not found in a place. Put an O in the box when you know where a mob was found.

- Neither the ender dragon nor the Enderman are near the end ship.
- Shulker is in the end city.
- Wither is not in the end city, the end gateway, or the exit portal.
- Ender dragon is in the exit portal.

	End City	End Ship	End Gateway	Exit Portal
ENDERMAN				
ENDER DRAGON				
SHULKER				
WITHER				

JUNGLE LOGIC

The jungle biome is a beautiful place to visit. If you keep your eyes open, you might find ocelots, parrots, pandas, and salmon. Use logic and the clues to figure out where you can spot each of these animals and what they might drop.

Hint: Put an X in the box when you know that an animal was not found in a place. Put an O in the box when you know where an animal was found.

- There is only one logical place to find salmon.

- The ocelot is one of the few mobs that drops nothing.

- The parrot has the best view of the jungle, and there is only one logical thing it could drop.

- Panda was not in the tall grass.

- The mob on the log drops bamboo.

	High in a Tree	On a Log	In the River	In the Tall Grass	BONE	NOTHING	FEATHER	BAMBOO
OCELOT								
PARROT								
PANDA								
SALMON								

LOGIC IN THE DESERT

Steve killed four mobs and collected four drops while exploring the desert biome. He is trying to remember which drops came from which mobs and where they were killed. Use the clues to help Steve sort his victories.

- Witch was in the desert temple and it did not drop anything from a four-legged animal mob.

- The mob behind the cactus hops and did not drop leather.

- Llama was thirsty but did not drop either rotten flesh or raw meat.

- Husk's drop was rotten.

	Behind the Cactus	In a Pyramid	Desert Temple	By the Well	ROTTEN FLESH	LEATHER	SPIDER EYES	RAW MEAT
HUSK								
LLAMA								
WITCH								
RABBIT								

WHICH WEAPONS?

Read the clues to figure out the weapons. The first one is done for you.

1. This weapon is used for close, hand-to-hand combat to inflict a crushing blow.

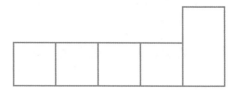

a	x	e

2. Also used for close, hand-to-hand combat, this weapon is used for a sweep attack.

3. This weapon cannot be crafted. It is a rare drop from a drowned. It must be thrown.

4. This weapon is shot from a bow and can cause status effects on mobs and players.

5. This weapon can launch arrows and fireworks great distances.

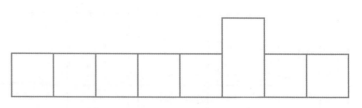

TOOL TIME

Read the clues to figure out the tools.

1. This is one of the most common tools used in Minecraft. It is used for mining ore and rock.

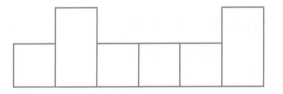

2. This tool helps the player collect dirt and other blocks.

3. This tool is used mostly for fishing.

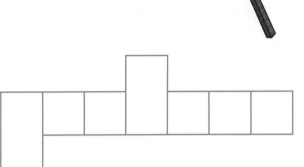

4. This tool is used to till dirt and grass block into farmland. It is also used to harvest some blocks.

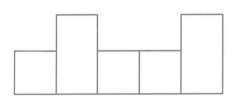

5. This tool is used to tell the sun and moon's position to the horizon.

MOB CATCHER

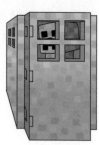

Read the directions to create a Mob Catcher. Then find a friend and play a game to see who can catch the most mobs.

HOW TO MAKE A MOB CATCHER

Step 1: Cut the Mob Catcher.

Step 2: Fold the square to make a triangle. Unfold. Fold again to make another triangle. Unfold. The creases should make an X in the center square.

Step 3: Flip the square so the words and numbers are face down. Fold each corner into the center.

Step 4: Flip the square over and fold all four corners to the center again.

Step 5: Fold the square in half so that you see the mobs on the outside.

Step 6: Insert two thumbs and two index fingers under the flaps with mobs and move your fingers back and forth to move the catcher.

HOW TO PLAY MOB CATCHER

Find a friend or family member to play with you. Take turns being Player 1 or 2.

PLAYER 1

1. Holds the Mob Catcher.

3. Spells the mob name, opening and closing the Mob Catcher.

5. Counts the number said, opening and closing the Mob Catcher.

7. Opens the flap and reads the outcome under the number said.

PLAYER 2

2. Names a mob.

4. Says a number.

6. Says another number.

MOB CATCHER

Cut out the Mob Catcher.

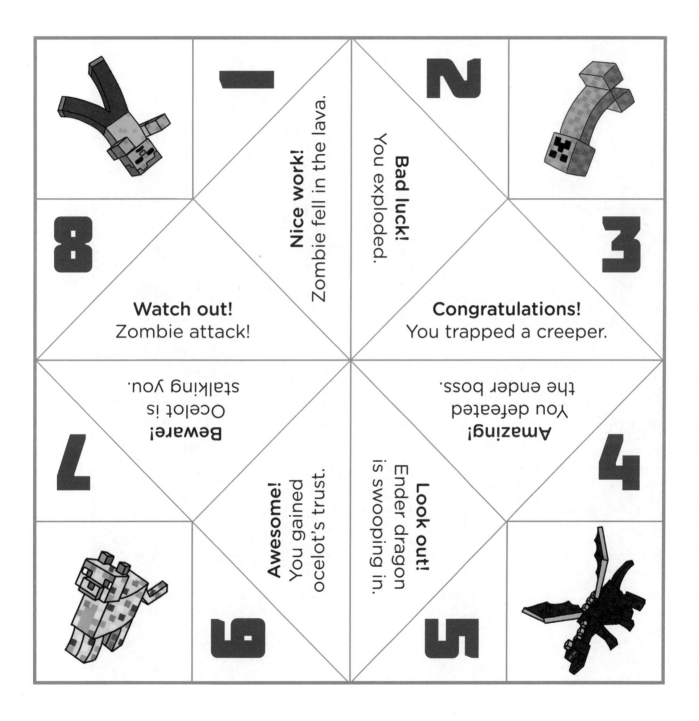

1

2

Nice work!
Zombie fell in the lava.

Bad luck!
You exploded.

8

3

Watch out!
Zombie attack!

Congratulations!
You trapped a creeper.

Beware!
Ocelot is stalking you.

Amazing!
You defeated the ender boss.

7

4

Awesome!
You gained ocelot's trust.

Look out!
Ender dragon is swooping in.

6

5

ANSWER KEY

PAGE 8

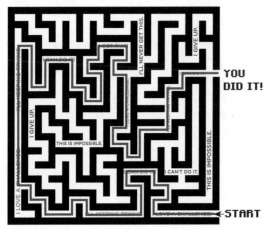

PAGE 27

Laugh at someone's JOKE.

SMILE at everyone you meet.

Make a CARD to thank someone for something they did for you.

Help a family member do his or her CHORES.

Share a SNACK with a friend.

COMPLIMENT someone on something they do

PAGE 33

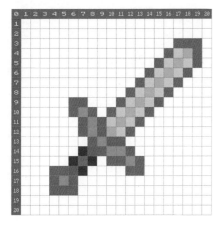

PAGE 55

PAGE 99

1. 5,633; 2. 2,061; 3. 7,280; 4. 3,491; 5. 9,120;
6. 8,576; 7. 1,999; 8. 4,003

PAGE 100

1. 4,894; 2. 5,001; 3. 4,000; 4. 6,822; 5. 1,740;
6. 7,014; 7. 9,002; 8. 8,221

PAGE 101

1. 400; 2. 6,000; 3. 3; 4. 800; 5. 1,000/50;
6. 900/90; 7. 3,000/1; 8. 2,000/800/30/4

PAGE 102

1. 85; 2. 72; 3. 79; 4. 67; 5. 98; 6. 66

PAGE 103

1. 88; 2. 87; 3. 99; 4. 65; 5. 97; 6. 63; 7. 93; 8. 98;
9. 86; 10. 89; 11. 79; 12. 77
FOR THE BROOM SERVICE

PAGE 104

1. 41; 2. 36; 3. 15; 4. 41; 5. 14; 6. 23

PAGE 105

1. 54; 2. 34; 3. 32; 4. 26; 5. 53; 6. 12; 7. 30; 8. 31;
9. 64; 10. 33; 11. 45; 12. 71
BLOCK THEIR PATH

PAGE 106

1. 52; 2. 72; 3. 41; 4. 95; 5. 70; 6. 82

PAGE 107

1. 60; 2. 86; 3. 83; 4. 101; 5. 95; 6. 85; 7. 105;
8. 110; 9. 71; 10. 81; 11. 84; 12. 72
BECAUSE IT HAS TEN-TICKLES

PAGE 108

1. 38; 2. 26; 3. 29; 4. 35; 5. 48; 6. 28

PAGE 109

1. 54; 2. 38; 3. 14; 4. 35; 5. 48; 6. 15; 7. 37; 8. 46; 9. 26
TO THE BAA BAA SHOP

PAGE 110

1. 52 plants; 2. 45 baby llamas;
3. 15 baby llamas; 4. 7 more diamonds

PAGE 111

1. 19 gems; 2. 102 gems; 3. 19 more diamonds;
4. 28 emeralds

PAGE 112

1. 64 spider legs; 2. 27 zombie villagers;
3. 42 skeletons; 4. 32 creepers

PAGE 113

1. 3 x 7 = 21; 2. 4 x 6 = 24; 3. 4 x 5 = 20;
4. 8 x 6 = 48; 5. 6 x 6 = 36; 6. 9 x 3 = 27

PAGE 114

x	0	1	2	3	4	5	6	7	8	9	10
0	0	0	0	0	0	0	0	0	0	0	0
1	0	1	2	3	4	5	6	7	8	9	10
2	0	2	4	6	8	10	12	14	16	18	20
3	0	3	6	9	12	15	18	21	24	27	30
4	0	4	8	12	16	20	24	28	32	36	40
5	0	5	10	15	20	25	30	35	40	45	50
6	0	6	12	18	24	30	36	42	48	54	60
7	0	7	14	21	28	35	42	49	56	63	70
8	0	8	16	24	32	40	48	56	64	72	80
9	0	9	18	27	36	45	54	63	72	81	90
10	0	10	20	30	40	50	60	70	80	90	100

PAGE 115

PAGE 116

A PORKYSPINE

PAGE 117

4 experience orbs

PAGE 118

HIDE IT UNDER CARPET

Friends won't see it but the effects will still work,
so they'll slip, bounce, or slooooooow down.

PAGE 119

9 zombie pigman spawn eggs

PAGE 120

1. 4 eggs; 2. 4 withers; 3. 6 melons; 4. 7 potions

PAGE 121

1. 8 diamonds; 2. 9 emeralds; 3. 9 tin ingots;
4. 6 gold ingots

PAGE 122

1. 21/3/7/21; 2. 54/6/9/54; 3. 56/7/8/56;
4. 48/6/8/48

PAGE 123

1. 12/4/3; 2. 42/7/6; 3. 40/5/8; 4. 36/4/9;
5. 35/5/7; 6. 45/9/5; 7. 24/6/4; 8. 63/7/9

PAGE 124

1. 10; 2. 20; 3. 30; 4. 40; 5. 50; 6. 60; 7. 70;
8. 80; 9. 90; 10. 100; 11. 110; 12. 120;
Add 0 in the ones place.

PAGE 125

1. 100; 2. 240; 3. 210; 4. 360; 5. 140; 6. 320;
7. 200; 8. 270; 9. 300; 10. 280; 11. 80; 12. 300;
13. 160; 14. 150; 15. 350; 16. 120

PAGE 126

1. 48; 2. 92; 3. 189; 4. 204; 5. 180; 6. 162; 7. 216;
8. 384; 9. 125; 10. 217; 11. 574; 12. 222

PAGE 127

1. 324; 2. 130; 3. 294; 4. 365; 5. 488; 6. 228;
7. 72; 8. 90; 9. 224; 10. 310; 11. 651; 12. 220; 13. 111;
14. 301; HE RUNS AROUND THE BLOCK.

PAGE 128

1. 40/4; 2. 80/8; 3. 30/9; 4. 60/6; 5. 60/6;
6. 70/7; 7. 90/9; 8. 70/7; 9. 80 / 8

PAGE 129

1. 6; 2. 9; 3. 6; 4. 4; 5. 6; 6. 9; 7. 3; 8. 7; 9. 8; 10. 7;
11. 9; 12. 3

PAGE 130

1. 8 R2; 2. 7; 3. 8 R3; 4. 6 R2; 5. 9 R1; 6. 9 R4;
7. 7 R5; 8. 6 R1; 9. 8 R4; 10. 3 R4; 11. 3 R3; 12. 6 R7

PAGE 131

1. 8 R3; 2. 5 R3; 3. 9 R6; 4. 7 R4; 5. 7; 6. 4 R5;
7. 6 R3; 8. 9 R5; 9. 6 R4; AT THE SPAWN SHOP

PAGE 132

1. 10, 14, 22, 24; 2. 8, 12, 24, 28, 40, 44;
3. 18, 36, 42, 54, 60; 4. 8, 32, 40, 48, 64, 88;
even 5. 15, 30, 35, 45, 50; 6. 21, 42, 56, 70;
7. 9, 36, 54, 63, 81, 99; both odd and even

PAGE 133

1. No, because 10 is not a multiple of 4;
2. 6, 12, 18, 24; 3. 12; 4. 10, 20; 5. 18, 36, 54; 6. 56

PAGE 134

SHIPWRECK, ICEBERG
SHIPWRECK is inside ICEBERG, one word inside another. In Minecraft, shipwrecks usually generate in oceans and on beaches, but occasionally they will generate in icebergs.

PAGE 135

11 sponge blocks

PAGE 136

PARKOUR

PAGE 137

30 - SNOW GOLEM

PAGE 138

PLANKS;
You'll hear mobs when they walk on them.

PAGE 139

9 beets

PAGE 140

A DEAD RINGER

PAGE 141

63 - BUFFET
You choose how a Buffet world is customized.

PAGE 142

"MOJANG" is a SWEDISH WORD meaning "GADGET." Mojang (pronounced "mo-YANG") is the name of the company that makes Minecraft.

PAGE 143

2 gold ingots

PAGE 144

52 - PISTON; A piston can be placed against a wall where you think a cave is hiding. If it pushes out, that means there might be a cave within 12 blocks. Dig for it!

PAGE 145

Use SIGNS and LADDERS to stop WATER and LAVA.

PAGE 146

PAGE 147

Alex calls her horse "Mayo," and SOMETIMES MAYO NEIGHS!

PAGE 148

48 - SILVERFISH

PAGE 149

FENCES make excellent DOORS
Zombies can't break the fences, and you can fight back through the fences. Genius!

PAGE 150

40 - CONDUIT

PAGE 151

PILLAR JUMPING - The pillar is placed while you're jumping.

PAGE 152

A BUCKET OF WATER

PAGE 153

6 flowers

PAGE 154

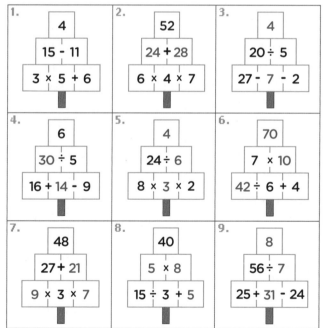

1. 4 / 15 - 11 / 3 × 5 + 6	2. 52 / 24 + 28 / 6 × 4 × 7	3. 4 / 20 ÷ 5 / 27 - 7 - 2
4. 6 / 30 ÷ 5 / 16 + 14 - 9	5. 4 / 24 ÷ 6 / 8 × 3 × 2	6. 70 / 7 × 10 / 42 ÷ 6 + 4
7. 48 / 27 + 21 / 9 × 3 × 7	8. 40 / 5 × 8 / 15 ÷ 3 + 5	9. 8 / 56 ÷ 7 / 25 + 31 - 24

PAGE 155

Diamond = 10
Bush = 6
Prismarine = 9
Ice = 8
Cobblestone = 3
Clay = 5
1. 63; 2. 480; 3. 4; 4. 6

PAGE 156

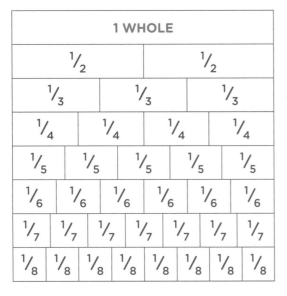

1 WHOLE							
$\frac{1}{2}$				$\frac{1}{2}$			
$\frac{1}{3}$		$\frac{1}{3}$			$\frac{1}{3}$		
$\frac{1}{4}$		$\frac{1}{4}$		$\frac{1}{4}$		$\frac{1}{4}$	
$\frac{1}{5}$	$\frac{1}{5}$		$\frac{1}{5}$		$\frac{1}{5}$		$\frac{1}{5}$
$\frac{1}{6}$	$\frac{1}{6}$	$\frac{1}{6}$	$\frac{1}{6}$		$\frac{1}{6}$		$\frac{1}{6}$
$\frac{1}{7}$	$\frac{1}{7}$	$\frac{1}{7}$	$\frac{1}{7}$	$\frac{1}{7}$	$\frac{1}{7}$		$\frac{1}{7}$
$\frac{1}{8}$	$\frac{1}{8}$	$\frac{1}{8}$	$\frac{1}{8}$	$\frac{1}{8}$	$\frac{1}{8}$	$\frac{1}{8}$	$\frac{1}{8}$

1. >; 2. =; 3. <; 4. <; 5. =; 6. <

PAGE 157

1. 3/8; 2. 5/8; 3. 2/8; 4. 2/8; 5. 2/8; 6. 2/8

PAGE 158

Shading of shapes will vary.

1. $\frac{6}{8}$ 2. $\frac{4}{6}$; 3. $\frac{4}{8}$; 4. $\frac{3}{12}$; 5. $\frac{2}{3}$; 6. $\frac{2}{8}$;

7. Two-eighths and one-fourth are equivalent fractions; they equal the same amount of pie. Eighths are smaller slices than fourths, so in this case, it's not true that 2 is more than 1.

PAGE 159

1. 2/6; 2. 4/8; 3. 6/10; 4. 4/8; 5. 3/6; 6. 5/5;
7. Multiplying by a fraction equal to 1.

PAGE 160

1. 5/8; 2. 7/8; 3. 4/8; 4. Find a common denominator and add the numerators.

PAGE 161

1. 2/8; 2. 3/8; 3. 3/8; 4. Find a common denominator and subtract the numerators.

PAGE 162

1. C; 2. A; 3. B; 4. D; 5. Divide the denominator into the numerator, then put the remainder over the denominator.

PAGE 163

I=20cm; L= 16cm; O= 16cm; V= 28cm; E= 24cm; M= 36cm; I= 12cm; N= 24cm; E= 24cm; C= 20cm; R= 20cm; A= 20cm; F= 20; T= 16cm

PAGE 164

1. 18cm; 2. 18cm; 3. 25cm; 4. 20cm; 5. 64cm;
6. 28cm; 7. The area of a rectangle is the length multiplied by the width.

PAGE 166

1. 2; 2. 2; 3. 1; 4. 1; 5. 1; 6. 2; 7. 2; 8. 2; 9. 3

PAGE 167

1. glow/stone; 2. laugh/ing; 3. spi/der; 4. ap/ple;
5.la/va; 6. craft/ed; 7. beet/root; 8. puff/er

PAGE 168

1. B; 2. A; 3. E; 4. C; 5. D

PAGE 169

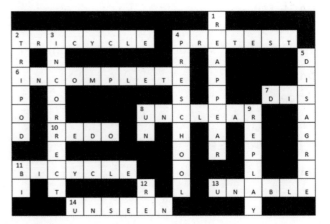

PAGE 170

1. invisible; can't see it
2. impossible; can't do
3. inedible; can't eat
4. disconnected; not connected
5. uninterested; not interested

PAGE 171

2. disappear; not there
3. incorrect; not right
4. insane; not sane
5. impatient; not patient
6. disagree; don't agree

PAGE 172

1. playful; 2. weaken; 3. careless; 4. avoidable

PAGE 173

1. sharpest; 2. faster; 3. darker; 4. coldest;
5. kindest; 6. longer

PAGES 174–175

1. discovery; 2. unpredictable; 3. uncomfortable;
4. disagreeable; 5. unlucky; 6. improperly;
7. unsuccessful

PAGE 176

PAGE 177

1. web; 2. light; 3. red; 4. stone; 5. puffer

PAGE 178

1. a sunken ship; 2. magical; 3. cutting tool;
4. continuing to live

PAGE 179

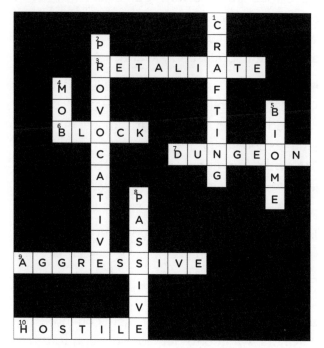

PAGE 180

1. for the good
2. to light up
3. changes
4. type

PAGE 181

A	P	A	S	S	I	V	E	M	O	D	B	I
G	E	S	U	R	V	I	V	A	L	P	H	O
G	H	A	R	M	F	U	L	L	T	O	N	E
R	O	E	P	O	T	I	O	N	S	T	V	L
E	S	A	B	E	N	E	F	I	C	I	A	L
S	T	I	L	O	I	M	E	V	N	O	R	N
S	I	V	B	I	O	M	E	C	E	N	I	E
I	L	A	I	V	M	O	B	R	A	T	A	T
V	E	S	U	N	D	E	A	D	S	F	N	H
E	C	R	E	A	T	I	V	E	T	E	T	E
I	L	L	U	M	I	N	A	T	E	B	E	R

PAGE 182

1. bat: a flying mammal / a stick used to hit a ball;
2. pen: an animal enclosure / a tool to write;
3. ring: the sound of a bell / a circular band; 4. fly:
an insect / to travel in the sky; 5. bark: the outer
layer of a tree / the sound a dog makes; 6. block:
a solid cube / to keep from passing; 7. sink: to go
below the water / a basin for water; 8. duck: an
animal that quacks / to move out of the way

PAGE 183

1. A; 2. B; 3. B; 4. B; 5. A; 6. A

PAGE 184

1. E; 2. G; 3. F; 4. A; 5. D; 6. H; 7. C; 8. B

PAGE 185

1. closed; 2. happy; 3. fast; 4. harm; 5. cold

PAGE 186

1. plants; 2. tools and weapons; 3. hostile mobs;
4. foods; 5. villagers; 6. passive mobs;
7. biomes; 8. potions; 9. drops

PAGE 187

1. snow; rocks; 2. spider; mobs that fly;
3. swing; things in a bedroom; 4. diamond;
liquids; 5. chicken; animals with four legs;
6. cobweb; weather; 7. ghast; mobs that swim

PAGE 188

1. Get the creeper to come into the trap. 2. Let
the creeper settle down. 3. Put a red flower on
one corner of the trap. 4. Put a yellow flower
on the opposite corner of the trap. 5. Open the
trap. 6. The creeper will follow you. 7. You now
have a tamed creeper.

PAGE 189

1. First, you'll need a shovel, some snow, a crafting table, and a pumpkin head. 2. Punch the snow with your shovel to make eight snowballs. 3. Put two snowballs in each of the two bottom left squares of the crafting table. 4. Then put two snowballs in each of the two middle left squares of the crafting table. 5. Now you have two snow blocks. 6. Put a pumpkin on top for the head.

PAGE 190

1. E; 2. D; 3. C; 4. B; 5. F; 6. A

PAGE 191

1. it turns into a zombie. 2. If a player is within 100 blocks of them, 3. make a gold axe. 4. When it is damaged by a player, 5. it grows into a bush. 6. When attacked,

PAGE 192

1. B; 2. C; 3. A; 4. B

PAGE 193

1. Main Idea: Llamas are useful desert mobs.
   Detail: They are neutral mobs that can be tamed.
   Detail: They are strong mobs that can carry heavy loads.
2. Main Idea: Husks are a type of zombie that lives in the desert.
   Detail: Husks do not burn in the sunlight.
   Detail: They avoid cliffs and water.
3. Main Idea: Desert biomes are large and lifeless.
   Detail: The surface is flat and sandy.
   Detail: Very few plants or animals live in the desert.

PAGE 194

1. spider; 2. bat; 3. guardian; 4. mooshroom; 5. turtle; 6. ocelot

PAGE 195

1. Steve went to the mine to find supplies for his project.
2. A bug stung him.
3. Steve shouted "Eureka!" when he found gold.
4. Steve crafted a golden sword.

PAGE 196

Main Ideas: Zombies are a common hostile mob in the Minecraft world.
Husks are a hostile mob and variant zombies that live in the desert.
Details will vary.

PAGE 197

Answers may vary but could include...
On zombies side: green body; colorful clothing; attack snow golems; can spot player from far away; burn in daylight; sink in water; drop head
On husks side: brown body; brown clothing; stomp on turtle eggs; can cause hunger; do not burn in sunlight; drop rotten flesh; can become a drowned; don't drop head
In intersection: groan; block body; two arms and legs; wear similar clothing style; hostile mob; attack players, villagers, iron golems, and baby turtles; avoid cliffs and lava; drop carrot or potato

PAGE 198

1. Drowned are underwater zombies. 2. They walk and swim underwater. They may step on land but will quickly look for nearby water. 3. a. to rise above water; b. close-range attacks; c. enemy

PAGE 199

1. Skeleton develops his skills. 2. He ran stairs; climbed ladders; ran through a maze; practiced archery and strafing; worked out in a lake. 3. a. sport using bow and arrows; b. fighting, jabbing in a circle; c. working hard

PAGE 200

1. wolf; 2. Wolf is angry; 3. Don't let your anger get the best of you.

PAGE 201

1. villagers; 2. zombie attacks; 3. to bell the zombies so they could hear them coming; 4. No one wanted to get close enough to the zombies to bell them. 5. You need to find a solution that is realistic.

PAGE 203

1. the unusual creeper; 2. friendly, happy, creative, loving; 3–4. Answers will vary.

PAGE 205

1. early morning in a village in the forest
2. It was dark and quiet. There was a cliff on one side and a lake on the other.
3. Answers will vary.

PAGE 207

Title: In the Jungle; Characters: Steve, parrot, ocelot; Setting: in the jungle; Beginning: Steve explores the jungle; Middle: Steve finds a parrot who helps him spot an ocelot; Ending: Steve, the parrot, and the ocelot explore the jungle together.

PAGE 210

1. thunder; 2. wind; 3. hail; 4. snow; 5. rain; 6. lightning; 7. temperature; 8. cloud

PAGE 211

1. A: 20, P: 24; 2. A: 12, P: 22; 3. A: 25, P: 30; 4. A: 24, P: 36

PAGE 212

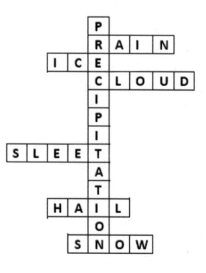

PAGE 213

1. on the farm; 2. in the jungle; 3. in the jungle and in the mountains; 4. at the swamp

PAGE 214

1. E; 2. D; 3. B; 4. F; 5. C; 6. A

PAGE 215

1. to create light; 2. to cook; 3. to grow; 4. to stay warm; 5. It will melt. 6. It will die.

PAGE 216

1. no; 2. yes; 3. yes; 4. yes; 5. no

PAGE 217

Pictures will vary.
1. Waves will be low and wide.
2. Waves will be high and close together.

PAGE 218

1. anvil; 2. pull; 3. feather; 4. downhill

PAGE 219

Answers will vary. Possible answers:
1. Putting an object in front of the spider
2. Gravity causes the ball to come back down.
3. The bones cause friction.
4. They will crash.

PAGE 220

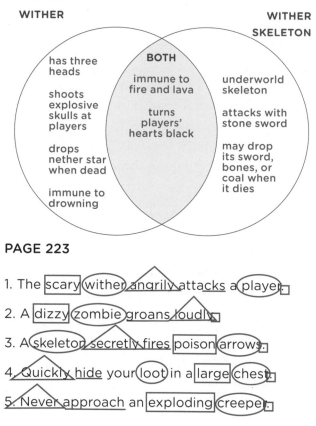

PAGE 223

1. The scary wither angrily attacks a player.
2. A dizzy zombie groans loudly.
3. A skeleton secretly fires poison arrows.
4. Quickly hide your loot in a large chest.
5. Never approach an exploding creeper.

PAGE 224

2. Horses eat carrots. Steve eats cake.
3. Alex rides a pig. Baby zombies ride chickens.
4. Creepers dance to the music. Creeper explodes on the player.

PAGE 225

1. are; 2. become; 3. wears; 4. do; 5. trade; 6. like

PAGE 226

1. builds; 2. attacks; 3. shoots; 4. teleport; 5. swims

PAGE 227

2. To make your flowers grow, place them in bonemeal.

3. The Enderman teleports over to Steve.

4. The players make a fishing rod from sticks and string.

5. The witches throw a splash potion.

6. The skeleton shoots many arrows.

7. The zombie prefers to live in the dark.

8. The jungle biomes have a lot of trees.

PAGE 228

2. Steve and Alex like to mine for diamonds.

3. End dragon and blaze fly. 4. The potion of invisibility and the potion of healing have positive effects. 5. The ocelot and parrot can be found in the jungle.

PAGE 229

2. Witch lives in the village and makes many potions. 3. Skeleton chased the player and shot him with his arrow. 4. Spider crawled up the wall and through the cobweb. 5. Nitwit has no job and wanders through the village.

PAGE 230

2. Alex's shirt is green.

3. Steve's magnet is strong.

4. The witch's hut is in the forest.

5. The thief's mask is black.

6. The zombie's clothes are ripped.

PAGE 231

2. the witches' potions

3. the mushrooms' spots

4. the sheep's wool

5. the people's city

PAGE 232

1. "Do you have anything to trade?" asked the villager.

2. Alex ran from the creeper yelling, "It's gonna blow!"

3. "Steve," said Alex, "I think it's time to explore the Nether."

4. When they dodged her splash potion, the witch yelled, "I'll get you next time."

5. "This is bad," said the zombie when it noticed the sun coming out.

PAGE 233

1. "What a beautiful emerald," said Steve.

2. "Let's go looking✗ for tonight's dinner," said Alex.

3. "Quick! Get your bow and arrow✗," Steve yelled.

4. "I want to be a chicken jockey when I grow up," said the baby zombie.✗

5. "I have a new diamond chest plate," Steve told Alex.

PAGES 234–235

1. their; 2. there; 3. their; 4. they're; 5. its; 6. It's; 7. it's; 8. two; 9. too; 10. to; 11. two, to; 12. loose; 13. lose

PAGES 236–237

1. well; 2. good; 3. your; 4. You're; 5. than; 6. then; 7. This; 8. That; 9. Those; 10. these; 11. accept; 12. except

PAGE 238

Answers will vary.

PAGE 239

1. ran, quickly; 2. fought, bravely; 3. carefully, crafted; 4. shone, brightly; 5. laughed, loudly; 6. spun, rapidly; 7. marched, randomly; 8. grew, tall/straight

PAGE 244

Minecraft is the video game (that) most kids play.

Minecraft, (which) can be played in Survival Mode or Creative Mode, is exciting.

Pigs are animals (that) can be tamed with a carrot.

Is (that) the mob that chased you?

The Enderman (that) finishes first wins the race.

The player (who) built the snow golem is very clever.

That's the chest (which) holds her armor.

That's the player (whose) armor is gold.

PAGE 245

1. Alex is the girl ___who___ is hugging the pig.
2. The diamond ___that___ Alex is holding is shiny.
3. The diamond sword ___that___ Steve made is very sharp.
4. The witch ___whose___ potion I used is wearing a purple robe.
5. The villager ___who___ grew the glistening melon is a good farmer.

PAGE 246

2. The villagers are waiting to trade.
3. Alex is riding in her minecart.
4. The chicken is laying eggs.
5. I am playing Minecraft with my friends.

PAGE 247

2. The ghasts were throwing fireballs as they attacked.
3. Alex was smiling as she crafted a golden sword.
4. The creeper was plotting revenge while he was in the trap.
5. The torches were lighting the way as Steve entered the cave.

PAGE 248

2. The bat will be flying tonight.
3. I will be looking for some blaze powder to make a potion.
4. The ghast will be shooting fireballs at the player in a race later today.
5. Steve will be crafting a diamond sword next week.

PAGE 249

1. P; 2. N; 3. P; 4. N; 5. P; 6. P

PAGE 254

1. 5; 2. 3; 3. 1; 4. 4; 5. 2

PAGE 260

___S___ 1. The endermite was as <u>quiet as a mouse</u>.
___S___ 2. The lava was <u>hot like the sun</u>.
___ 3. The shovel was very sharp.
___S___ 4. The zombies were as <u>green as spring grass</u>.
___S___ 5. Steve slept <u>like a baby</u>.
___ 6. The sheep is dyed bright pink.

PAGE 261

___M___ 1. She is a prickly cactus.
___M___ 2. He was a pig at dinner.
___M___ 3. My brother is a couch potato.
___ 4. The ghast was so angry that it screamed.
___ 5. That evoker is a real ogre.
___M___ 6. The sun was shining brightly.

PAGE 262

2. A; 3. C; 4. E; 5. F; 6. D

PAGE 263

2. G; 3. E; 4. C; 5. F; 6. A; 7. B

PAGES 266–267

1. The creeper has block-shaped feet. It is green.
2. Steve likes to tame wolves to keep as pets. He puts red collars on them.
3. Alex fought the wither with all her strength. Her bow and arrow came in very handy.
4. The player was very sneaky. He stole everything out of my chest.
5. Alex uses a pickaxe to mine for diamonds. She will make a diamond sword when she is done.
6. Steve made eye contact with the Enderman. The Enderman teleported toward him.
7. Diamond swords are very useful. They can destroy blazes, Endermen, and zombies.
8. Building a house in Minecraft is fun. You must add doors to keep out hostile mobs.

PAGE 271

1. Alex's cow and chicken had fun on the farm.
2. Librarian's favorite book is <u>The Atlas of Minecraft Biomes</u>.
3. "Here is a poppy for you," said iron golem to the villager.
4. Will snow golem melt on a hot sunny day?
5. Steve captured creeper on Tuesday and put it in a trap.

PAGE 289

1. GOLD INGOT; 2. HAY BALE; 3. SPIDER; 4. REDSTONE DUST; THE HORNED SHEEP

PAGE 290

U	S	E		Q	R		C	O	D	E	S
		T	O		I	N	V	I	T	E		F
R	I	E	N	D	S		T	O		B	U
I	L	D		W	I	T	H		Y	O	U

PAGE 291

1. SHOVEL; 2. CACTUS; 3. WOLF; 4. ELYTRA;
THEY HAVE TWO LEFT FEET!

PAGE 292

F	I	R	E		S	P	R	E	A	
D	S		F	A	S	T	E	R		
I	N		M	I	N	E	C	R	A	
F	T		E	A	R	T	H		T	
H	A	N		O	T	H	E	R		
V	E	R	S	I	O	N	S		O	
F		T	H	E		G	A	M	E	

PAGE 293

1. COOKIE; 2. ROTTEN FLESH; 3. ARROW;
4. MUDDY PIG; DON'T TAKE ME FOR GRANITE

PAGE 294

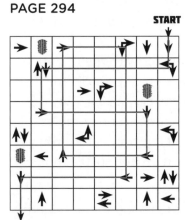

PAGE 295

```
M M O O B L O M O O
O O M L O B O O M B
M M O O O B L O O M
B O L M O M L O B O
M M O O L B M L L O
B O L L O O O B O L
L B B O B O O O O B
O M M L M O M B M O
O M O O L B O M O M
M O O L O B O M M L
```

PAGE 296

E	A	R	N		E	X	P	E	R	I	E
N	C	E		P	O	I	N	T	S		W
I	T	H		T	A	P	P	A	B	L	E
S		T	O		L	E	V	E	L		U
P		A	N	D		U	N	L	O	C	K
	B	U	I	L	D	P	L	A	T	E	S

PAGE 297

1. DRUMSTICK; 2. FISHING POLE; 3. BEACON;
4. LAPIS LAZULI; BUILDPLATES CAN BE
GRIEFED. So invite friends you trust.

PAGE 298

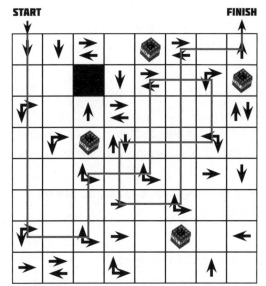

PAGE 299

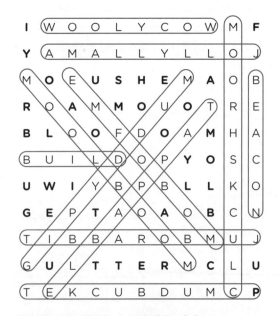

IF YOU SHEAR A MOOBLOOM,
YOU WILL GET A BUTTERCUP.

PAGE 300

START   FINISH

PAGE 301

1. DONKEY; 2. BUTCHER; 3. WOOLLY COW;
4. DIAMONDS; WATER CAN DESTROY A MUD
SOURCE BLOCK

PAGE 302

They come on COMMAND. Get it? Illusioners
don't spawn naturally, but you can make them
spawn with the /summon illusioner command.

PAGE 303

A player in a minecart on a rail can ride
THROUGH A ONE-BLOCK WALL

PAGE 304

4 enchanted books

PAGE 305

ENDERMEN

PAGE 306

35 - I NEED OARS

PAGE 307

NEVER DIG DOWN

PAGE 308

Use cobwebs to create delays in REDSTONE
CIRCUITS.

PAGE 309

ALWAYS MOVE WEST

PAGE 310

12 guardians

PAGE 311

ITEM FRAMES

PAGE 312

9 creepers

PAGE 313

HE CAME TO A BED END.

PAGE 314

12 slime blocks

PAGE 315

Mine SAND and GRAVEL with TORCHES.

PAGE 316

describe; scribe; crib; cry; try

PAGE 317

niece; wince; since; singe; sing

PAGE 318

1. 7 diamond blocks; 2. 16 diamonds and 8 sticks;
3. 8 diamond axes; 4. 31 diamonds and 24 sticks

PAGE 319

1. 8x4=32 boots/ 8x8=64 chest plates/ 5x8=40
helmets/ 7x8=56 leggings; 2. 40÷4=10 boots
or 40÷8=5 chest plates or 40÷5=8 helmets or
40÷7=5 leggings

PAGE 320

1. gold block; 2. gold ingot; 3. 45; 4. 162

PAGE 321

1. gold pickaxe; 2. 11 gold ingots and 12 sticks;
3. 3 gold hoes/ 1 gold pickaxe and 2 gold shovels

PAGE 322

PAGE 323

PAGE 324

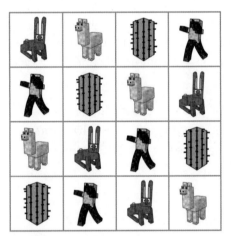

PAGE 325

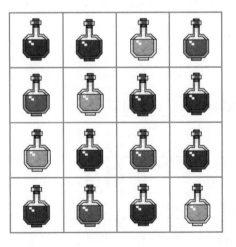

PAGE 326

BECAUSE IT IS A BOAR.

PAGE 327

1. AT THE MEAT BALL; 2. HIP HOP

PAGE 328

1. THE LIVING ROOM; 2. DEAD PAN

PAGE 329

1. NOBODY KNOWS; 2. SPARE RIBS

PAGES 330-331

1. BEETS ME; 2. FROM SCRATCH;

3. ROOST BEEF; 4. FOUL WEATHER;

5. IT'S HERD IT ALL; 6. A NIGHTMARE

PAGE 332

PAGE 334

	In the Garden	In the Tall Grass	In the Mushroom Field	In the Barn
COW	X	O	X	X
MOOSHROOM	X	X	X	O
MOOBLOOM	X	X	O	X
SUNSET COW	O	X	X	X

PAGE 335

	End City	End Ship	End Gateway	Exit Portal
ENDERMAN	X	X	O	X
ENDER DRAGON	X	X	X	O
SHULKER	O	X	X	X
WITHER	X	O	X	X

PAGE 336

Ocelot is in the tall grass, drops nothing.
Parrot is high in a tree, drops a feather.
Panda is on a log, drops bamboo.
Salmon is in the river, drops a bone.

PAGE 337

Husk was in the pyramid and dropped rotten flesh.
Llama was by the well and dropped leather.
Witch was in the desert temple and dropped spider eyes.
Rabbit was behind the cactus and dropped raw meat.

PAGE 338

1. axe; 2. sword; 3. trident; 4. arrow; 5. crossbow

PAGE 339

1. pickaxe; 2. shovel; 3. fishing rod; 4. hoe; 5. clock

Cut the cards and use with the Zombies Bounce Back Game on pages 38–39.

Zombies have attacked! **Bounce Back!** or Move back one space.	Zombies have broken down the door! **Bounce Back!** or Move back three spaces.	The sun rose on a zombie. They are near death. **Help it Bounce Back!** or Move back one space.	Zombies attacked the villagers. **Help the villagers Bounce Back!** or Move back three spaces.
You killed a zombie. It dropped a piece of rotten flesh. You get food poisoning. **Bounce Back!** or Move back one space.	You get trapped in a zombie mob spawner. **Bounce Back!** or Move back one space.	Zombie is teased about its green skin color. **Help it Bounce Back!** or Move back three spaces.	Zombie is teased about its clothes. **Help it Bounce Back!** or Move back one space.
Zombie is moaning about being lonely. **Help it Bounce Back!** or Move back three spaces.	Baby zombie is crying. **Help it Bounce Back!** or Move back one space.	Zombie is picked last for a game because it is so slow. **Help it Bounce Back!** or Move back three spaces.	Baby zombie is stuck in a block. **Help it Bounce Back!** or Move back one space.
Baby zombie is sad because it won't grow into an adult zombie. **Help it Bounce Back!** or Move back one space.	You were defeated by a zombie. How embarrassing. **Bounce Back!** or Move back three spaces.	You shot a zombie with an arrow. Now they are attacking! **Bounce Back!** or Move back three spaces.	Zombie lost its gear. It is sad. **Help it Bounce Back!** or Move back one space.
Zombie broke its sword. It is mad. **Help it Bounce Back!** or Move back three spaces.	Lucky you! You found a baby zombie on a chicken. Move forward one space.	Lucky you! You destroyed the zombie. Move forward one space.	Lucky you! You found a cave filled with gems after following a zombie moan. Move forward three spaces.

BOUNCE BACK	BOUNCE BACK	BOUNCE BACK	BOUNCE BACK
BOUNCE BACK	BOUNCE BACK	BOUNCE BACK	BOUNCE BACK
BOUNCE BACK	BOUNCE BACK	BOUNCE BACK	BOUNCE BACK
BOUNCE BACK	BOUNCE BACK	BOUNCE BACK	BOUNCE BACK
BOUNCE BACK	BOUNCE BACK	BOUNCE BACK	BOUNCE BACK